I0797389

CHOREPLAY

CHOREPLAY

The Marriage-Saving Magic of Getting Your Head Out of Your Ass

JORDAN CARLOS

GRAND CENTRAL
New York Boston

Cover design by Albert Tang
Cover art by Doug Chayka

Grand Central Publishing
Hachette Book Group
1290 Avenue of the Americas
New York, NY 10104
grandcentralpublishing.com
@grandcentralpub

First Edition: February 2026

Grand Central Publishing is a division of Hachette Book Group, Inc.
The Grand Central Publishing name and logo are registered trademarks of Hachette Book Group, Inc.

Print book interior design by Bart Dawson.

Library of Congress Cataloging-in-Publication Data

Name: Carlos, Jordan author
Title: Choreplay: the marriage-saving magic of getting your head out of your ass / Jordan Carlos.
Description: First edition. | New York: Grand Central Publishing, 2026. | Includes bibliographical references.
Identifiers: LCCN 2025026713 | ISBN 9780306836138 hardcover | ISBN 9780306836145 trade paperback | ISBN 9780306836152 ebook
Subjects: LCSH: Husbands | Husbands—Humor | Marriage
Classification: LCC HQ756 .C365 2026
LC record available at https://lccn.loc.gov/2025026713

ISBNs: 978-0-306-83613-8 (hardcover), 978-0-306-83615-2 (ebook)

Printed in Canada

MRQ-T

10 9 8 7 6 5 4 3 2 1

First, I want to thank me for writing this book.
Thanks, pal. Ya did it! No one thought we could.
(That's obviously something I just made up,
'cause I love to cast myself as a scrappy underdog.)

Next, I want to thank my wife for being game for building
a life with a comedian. You are why I wrote this book.
I have loved you since I met you in that Manhattan
nightclub (back when you could do that!) on
Fourth Ave. and Thirteenth Street.

Also, I dedicate this book to my dynamic
and amazing children, Izzy and Malcolm.
You inspire me to do more and be more.

And I cannot forget my parents—Joe and Hazel—
for teaching me how to love with all my heart.

Special shouts, of course, to my siblings, too.
I see you. I love you.

EPIGRAPH

"Long Friday"

QUICK STORY.

On Friday, October 24, 1975, nine out of ten women in Iceland took a day off.[1] Was it a major holiday? No. But women refused to do any work—paid or unpaid—for the day. They did not show up for their jobs in any sector, including offices, factories, schools, hospitals, police departments, construction sites, day cares, and nursing homes. That day, Icelandic women took to the streets in mass protest. Thing is, putting down the laundry baskets and kitchen knives, and the diapers too, they also did not show up domestically. No biggie, right?

Iceland was brought to its knees. Full stop. Life on the island nation came to a complete standstill. Men across the country scrambled to fill in for their partners, taking their children to work with them because day care centers were closed and wives refused to do everything else. The restaurants that somehow managed to remain open were inundated with men suddenly overwhelmed by the stress of having to feed their kids and themselves. The nationwide protest, known as "Women's Day Off" or "The Long Friday," effectively cut Iceland off from the rest of the world.[2] Calls literally could not come in or go out because women usually "manned" the switchboards. Planes could not take off or land at the country's airports. Male TV news anchors had to corral their rambunctious children while also trying to do live TV news broadcasts since they had no choice but to bring the kiddos to work that day. For the men of Iceland, it was a goddamn catastrophe and a total reversal of fortunes. But, hey, they'd had a good run, right?

The Women's Day Off was no fluke. It proved to be more than just a one-off booty call demonstration. Its impact on Icelandic society was enormous.[3] Five years after the Women's Day Off protest, Iceland would go on to democratically elect the first female president in history, Vigdís Finnbogadóttir, who would not only serve four consecutive terms but also, in her tenure, play a key diplomatic role in ending the Cold War.[4] Moreover, after the protest, Iceland would adopt laws to better ensure gender equity in the workplace, such as everyone getting paid the same amount for doing the same job no matter their gender (duh) and paid family leave—two things the USA *still* doesn't have at the federal level, as of this writing.[5]

Long Friday illustrates the folly of willfully ignoring certain people's contributions and efforts relative to others'. Eventually, there is a correction.

The trick is to not get caught on the wrong side.

CONTENTS

LEVEL TWO

FINAL BOSS LEVEL

FOREWORD

by Charlamagne Tha God

Let me tell y'all something right now: this book you're holding? IT WILL NOT SAVE YOUR MARRIAGE. I repeat, IT WILL NOT SAVE YOUR MARRIAGE.

The Lebron James Version of the Bible says faith without works is dead! That basically means faith is not just a belief, but it also involves actions that demonstrate that belief. So, if you think this book is going to save your marriage without you putting in the work to save your marriage, then stop reading right now! But if you're ready to work, don't judge a book by its cover. This is not about mops, buckets, and Windex. This is a damn marriage manual disguised as a comedy special. A Trojan Swiffer, if you will.

When my friend Jordan Carlos (whom I have affectionately called "Counsel" for the last decade plus) sent me the early pages of *Choreplay*, I read it and laughed out loud A LOT. Then I looked around the kitchen like, damn... when was the last time I unloaded that dishwasher? See, this book is going to make you want to do the WORK to ensure you have the marriage you both deserve—it's funny, but it hits home like a passive-aggressive Post-it on the mirror.

Listen, I've been married for eleven years, but I've been with my wife for twenty-seven years. (Don't you dare fucking judge me,

High School Sweethearts have to grow into adulthood!) But trust me when I tell you, it's not the big stuff that tests your love—it's the little things. Building a life with someone is the ultimate compromise, and you cannot all of a sudden develop selective blindness when you decide to live happily ever after with a person. In fact, you have to learn to see what's not visible to the naked eye. You have to know what your wife wants to eat when you ask her "What do you want to eat?" and she replies "You choose." And you have to deal with the fact that whatever you order, she really won't be happy with! I know, I know. That makes absolutely no sense, but guess what? NEITHER DOES MARRIAGE!!!!

Jordan's got jokes, but this isn't a stand-up routine—it's relationship CPR. It's a wakeup call for every man who thinks doing the bare minimum is "helping out," and every woman who's been silently screaming, "Why do I feel like your mom instead of your wife?!"

Loving someone and wanting to spend the rest of your life with them is genuine Insanity, but when it works, it works—and it won't work if you don't do the work. That's what *Choreplay* is all about.

Enjoy. Like I did.

—Lenard "Charlamagne Tha God" McKelvey

CHOREPLAY

INTRODUCTION

FAME IS A WICKED MISTRESS. SHE'S SUBJECT TO WHIMSY AND, as is often the case, the vicissitudes of an algorithm. Case in point, there's a dad in my friend circle who is famous among a certain collection of Brooklyn moms for making his wife coffee *every* morning and bringing it to her in bed. That's sweet, isn't it? It's the kind of thing Olds do in movies, right? But let's unpack that for a moment, 'cause it bears repeating.

The guy is *F-A-M-O-U-S* for making his wife a single cup of coffee every morning! No croissant and jam, no Denver omelet on the side. Just a cup of java in her favorite mug—allegedly. Think for a moment how low the bar for cisgender, straight dudes must be when you achieve notoriety in your peer group for simply making your spouse a cup of Folgers Crystals in the morning. I mean, *yikes*. And this guy I am talking about is also Canadian, so *of course he makes coffee for his wife*!

The Canadian coffee maneuver always seemed like something of a joke to me—a middle-aged male trying to do way too much and, in so doing, making the rest of us look bad. But then, after I had one too many brushes with divorce, suddenly, coffee sounded like a swell idea!

One night, after a lengthy "exchange of hot marital takes" with Wife (read: all-out verbal, Vietnam-type firefight, where the d-word got tossed around like a sock in a dryer), I thought, "What would Canada Dad do?" He'd make morning coffee! That's what he'd do!

Now, I don't actually drink coffee, per se (because I think I'm better than ~~the weak-willed who need caffeine to function~~ everyone), so that was a bit of a setback, but I could *make* coffee!

I went to YouTube and was like, "YouTube, do your thing!" Morning coffee truly felt like *the* relationship save… until I realized just how much of a pain in the ass that would be for me. Where to start, folks?!

First, if I wanted to brew my wife a pot of morning coffee, it meant I'd have to either program our Mr. Coffee coffeemaker the night before (sounds like a lot of work) or wake up early to make the coffee. Oof! *Wake up early? Me?*

Full disclosure: For a long time, this stand-up comedian didn't even so much as set an alarm. I woke up when my wife told me to… you know, like a kid. I was shocked at how trying to do something as seemingly basic as making morning coffee for my spouse in the hopes of saving my sputtering marriage suddenly became as stressful as folding a fitted sheet.

The mere attempt to make morning brew exposed so much about me *to me*, and none of it was good; namely, I was an insomniac manchild who lacked the motivation and wherewithal to rise, despite the stakes. So, kudos to Canada Dad, 'cause this morning coffee shit wasn't as easy as it looked.

Suffice it to say, despite my general lazy-assed lethargy, I pulled myself out of my bed like Rocky Balboa at the end of *Rocky II* when he's trying to climb the ropes after both he and Apollo Creed full-on knock each other to the canvas and must rise before the referee can count to ten. Half-blind and drowsy, I scoured the kitchen for filters and beans until I was able to muster some decent-to-palatable joe. I steamed the whole milk on the stove and frothed it to silken effervescence. After adding just enough agave, I chose her go-to mug and tiptoed into our room.

I found my wife sleeping deeply (shout-out to sleeping aids). She looked so beautiful, so unbothered. Nervous, I waved the steaming cup under her nostrils. They flared. Was she pissed? Did I burn the coffee?

After a beat, I saw something wild. A smile! She slid off her sleeping mask, looked at the coffee, and then took me in. It was a start.

As I went back downstairs, I smiled at my minor win. I knew I had to do more than just make coffee. I thought to myself, "How can I scale this idea?" My problems were not going to be solved with a fancy bag of Ethiopian Yirgacheffe. *If only*...

But that cup of coffee was a flashpoint for me. If I could make my wife coffee in the morning, what else could I do? What else was I not doing? What else was I leaving up to her? The answer, as you will see, to put it in super-fancy scientific terms—a buttload.

Now, from what I've noted from my experience, and from what I've observed in my friend circles (aka more super-scientific research), it actually doesn't take all that much for a marriage to fall off like your favorite K-pop boy band. Based mainly on what I've seen on WhatsApp mom chats, romantic love tends to buy you up to ten years—*tops!*—of great-to-serviceable matrimony. I say this having gone to enough ten-year-anniversary shindigs where the after-party goes down in divorce court. But according to the 2021 US Census Bureau report, the average American marriage that ends in divorce lasted eight years.[1] And who you gonna believe—*the gubment??* Don't answer that...

While the first ten years of marriage are far from cake, that second decade is akin to a Fallujah firefight. Because, in all likelihood, the second ten years of marriage will probably include—in no particular order—kid(s), mortgage(s), career highs (and lows), credit card debt, death(s), costly car repairs, taxes, miscarriages (we don't talk about those!), out-of-network couples therapy (aka can we just break up 'cause that would be cheaper), and too much Disney Plus. To make it through this gauntlet only lightly maimed, men need to update their entire marriage operating system. I mean, we all have to update our phone software every couple of hours, so this shouldn't be too tough, right?

What it actually takes to dead a marriage isn't as salacious as all that. Lucky for us, it can be pretty basic and quotidian. In fact, according to a 2013 report that was featured by the

National Library of Medicine (let's call it my fave repository of scientific literature), three out of every four people in a sample of 306 ranked lack of commitment (or, showing the eff up daily) as the prevailing reason for their divorce, exceeding infidelity.[2] I'll leave that right there.

So, arguably speaking, there's a 75 percent chance that what ends a marriage may well be that pile of clothes that we leave at the foot of our bed, despite our person's repeated pleas to put them away. Or the door that we never get around to fixing, the trash that we never take out, the leaves we never rake, or the grass we (you see the pattern here) never cut unless asked to do so. Such little things, but on a long enough timeline, they will push marriages (read: my marriage) to the brink. Sounds dumb and anticlimactic, right? Well, life ain't Netflix.

Honestly, I'd wager a lot of cis, straight dudes aren't really taught the insidious danger inherent in constantly being reminded to straighten or tidy, especially if you're willing to do it when asked. For a long time I thought just being willing to hop to was enough. Turns out, it ain't. And also, who has the time to be this engaged? Shocker: You do, though it might not seem like it, and we'll get to that too.

What it took to turn my marriage around was a keen awareness of my wife's feelings (can't stress that enough!) PLUS, as strange as it sounds, a keen awareness of how much milk was in the fridge at any given time. When I started keeping track of things like milk or orange juice levels or when the kids needed to go to the dentist next, I could feel a shift. Doing the work in therapy was crucial, but also crucial was doing the literal work at home—the sorting, the organizing, and scrubbing that weird space behind the toilet, too. The one where angels dare not tread, dreams definitely go to die, and random yellow Lego heads find their final rest.

When I set out trying to up my game around the house, I felt like I was learning to walk all over again, like a toddling babe with bubbling lips and a full diaper. There was so much my wife knew about our home, our family, and our lives that I didn't. For instance, I am ashamed to say I didn't know the name of my kids' dentist. And though I dropped my kids off at school three times a week, I didn't know how to get in touch with their teachers. I wasn't really sure what after-school programs my kids were in or on what days those programs were happening. Basically, all I did was pay for said program and attend the recital. I also didn't know my kids' shoe sizes (they're always changing!), and I didn't know what size clothes they wore (also constantly changing!). So, not only was my wife responsible for knowing how much of each of these items we had/needed, she had to keep all of this top of mind while working a full-time job and raising two young kids.

But we haven't gotten to the worst part yet. The worst part is that, even given all this, I was considered one of the *good* dads. These aren't my words. I've heard moms say this about me in our circle between glasses of frosty rosé. Why? Because the bar was so low.

Now, some people may read this and think, *You're on easy street, dude. Shut your face hole before you ruin it for the rest of us.*

But in reality, that "good dad" tag was just a primrose path. I was setting up my marriage for a slowly gestating crash, and I was doing that by not being present in my home and by being little more than an emotional dependent—a kid who could drive and who made a good income, sure, but a kid nonetheless. My wife didn't sign up to marry an emotional child. No one goes into marriage hoping for that. Obviously, you want your person to grow along with you, not just get older while staying stuck. But that's what I was doing. I wasn't maturing—I was just accumulating years, responsibilities, and resentment. I mistook "providing" for participating. I thought showing up with a paycheck gave me moral cover for checking out emotionally. And for a while, that lie worked... until it didn't.

I wrote *Choreplay* to lead people away from the seductive trap of switching to relationship autopilot. My goal here—to quote the US Constitution—is to "create a more perfect union." Yeah, see, your union I'm sure is already *perfect.* We're just gonna make it "more perfect." Gotta love the Founding Fathers and their way with words.

To make this happen, we'll tackle as many problem areas and solutions as I could cram into these pages. We'll talk about getting to bed at a decent hour and waking up before dawn, the magic of functional exercise, and why picking up after yourself is more powerful than you think. We'll cover the importance of labeling what's yours, leaving your phone out of the bathroom, rethinking your devotion to a sports franchise that eats up your time, and—yes—joining Costco. These aren't radical changes, which is the best part. You'll see how small shifts can make a big difference in your marriage—in all areas of your relationship, especially the sex part.... I don't call it choreplay because it won't get you laid!

By the end, I hope *Choreplay* will alert you, dear reader, to the hazards of remaining on autopilot like I did. It will serve as a Jamaican air horn to change course before it's too late. Don't wind up like other men I know: cast aside (rightly so), broken, and quite literally living in their childhood room.

If you're down to save your relationship, and maybe dust a corner or two along the way, read on.

LISTEN UP. TIME IS NOT ON OUR SIDE, SO PLEASE TAKE A SEAT and keep all fingers and toes inside the cabin for the remainder of the flight. The goal of this book is to offer up simple/practical hacks for peaceful cohabitation with your person. To that end, we need to identify what we're up against.

We'll begin with a silent behemoth, "invisible work," a common yet unseen bit of nasty dysfunction that stripped the internal gears and wiring of my marriage, pushing it over the edge. When I saw it, I could not unsee it. I hope the same for you. We'll dive in and discuss how to actively see through this shroud of invisibility, then get the right tools to combat the threat. And after the outsides, we'll survey the insides. I'll share my ongoing fight to establish and maintain my own self-worth and how that factors in to my willingness to share in the chore work, which by the end of the book saves my marriage. It's all connected, y'all!

Somebody pass me a tweed jacket, I'm gonna slap on some elbow patches, 'cause it's time to go to Knowledge College!

Chapter 1

INVISIBLE WORK

Silent but Deadly AF

I WAS BORN INTO CAR CULTURE (STAY WITH ME HERE). SOME OF my earliest memories are of my brother and me playing "That's My Car" in my mom's wine-red, early-eighties Chevy Cavalier station wagon made of genuine DE-troit Steel. From times tables to Sunday school preparation (which was a thing in my house) to one-hand-on-the-wheel-while-other-hand-spanks, from family-wide firefights (read: "discussions") to flaming first kisses—on leather if you were lucky—it all went down in the car.

Wife, on the other hand, grew up navigating the chaotic 1980s New York subway: graffiti, crowds, catcalls, and all. Many New Yorkers are proud to say that they do not know how to drive—*'cause why learn?!* And though Wife definitely *can* drive, she mostly does not drive if we are traveling together. As a result, I am the de facto Lyft driver in our family.

This means I am generally responsible for all things car: timely transpo, navigation, gauging vital fluid levels like gas (sorry, Earth!) and oil (don't hate me, I'm going electric!). I'm also responsible for keeping an eye on driving time, playing amateur DJ (though Wife cringes when I manipulate the touchscreen whilst maneuvering city streets), and finally, perhaps the most nerve-shattering task of all in NYC, parallel parking. New Yorkers claim to be so busy, and yet they somehow find the time to form a small crowd near the curb in the hopes of witnessing drivers failing to squeeze their machines into a given parking spot.

While I am busy negotiating New York's treacherous arteries, many of which seem one pothole away from total collapse, Wife reclines in the passenger seat, entirely unbothered. She tunes out, feet up on the dash, blissfully unaware of the myriad split-second decisions, hairpin turns, or controlled baby driver skids required for an afternoon trip to Coney Island. When we arrive at our destination, I'm often a white-knuckled mess, pumping with adrenaline and desperately in need of the comforting mist of an inhaler. Wife is no worse for wear, chiller than a polar bear's toenails. Spa fresh, totally blissed.

All this to say, routines in relationships seemingly come out of nowhere. Driving my family around NYC is a stressful AF, often thankless gig that's somehow been left for me to do. Wife and I never established that I am the designated driver (again, to be clear, she can totally drive). We just somehow slipped into this pattern over our combined twenty years together, and much like the Ten Commandments or my Netflix password, it feels a little unalterable now. Even if I wanted to switch with her, it's hard to just tap out and swap drivers when you're barreling across the Brooklyn Bridge at rush hour. And whenever I do complain about always being the one behind the wheel, Wife hits me with the gaslight triple play: "Oh, you're so much better at driving than I am," or "I just love that you know your way around New York, and I can just zone out," or my favorite, "You just love to drive, though, right?" I mean, *yes*, I do *like* to drive, but who wants the stress all the time? Do I look like an air traffic controller? Don't answer that. My goofy-ass glasses don't help.

Beyond routine, my not-so-fun assignment as the family chauffeur is an example of "invisible work." These tasks are often grueling and repetitive, and unless I sell a sitcom called *How I Met Your Mothers—and Left the Others* that goes on for way too many seasons, I don't foresee giving up my role anytime soon. And like all invisible work, it's *unpaid*.

To be clear, I am not trying to garner sympathy here (though I will take it—praise me as the self-aware ally to women everywhere that I am!). Honestly, it's not uncommon for guys to do the lion's share of driving in straight relationships, so shout-outs to my fellow road warriors. I see you. I embrace your journey! Instead, I bring it up because it stands out as perhaps the most aggravating and, until very recently, possibly the *only chore* I was required to do. On the other hand, Wife was pretty much responsible for everything else!

Whether it's keeping track of how much milk, juice, or coffee is left, planning weekends or vacations, scheduling doctors' appointments, or determining which of our perpetually growing children's clothes need to be washed and/or given away, for the entirety of our marriage, she has been on it like a bonnet. By driving, I was literally saving her from doing it all, because it was literally the least I could do.

Now, before I further mansplain what invisible work is and what it isn't, I will say it should not be confused with "invisible twerk," which we all know is the twerking done by the ghosts and spirits who tragically did not get to twerk enough in their lifetimes. But, really, *invisible work* is just a fancy term for what used to be pejoratively known as "women's work" or "skirtwork." Our modern label is an umbrella term for all work having to do with the day-to-day operation of a household/family—biological or otherwise—including, but not limited to, cooking, cleaning, and laundry. It's called *invisible* because this labor goes unnoticed and/or is disregarded, and it definitely does not factor into a country's overall GDP. It's also called the "second shift," so named because it's literally a whole-ass second shift of work a woman must do when she gets home from her first shift, aka her paycheck.

If you think this doesn't seem like enough reason to make your wife coffee, consider the following. If American women were paid minimum wage for the unpaid care work they do around the house—the cooking and cleaning, bathing kids, nursing elderly and infirm adults—they would have made $1.5 trillion last year.[1] Some of y'all might even know all this from trying to get a nanny or even a sitter for the night. Childcare is a total flex! I've paid the neighbor kid $25 per hour just to watch my kids for a date night. It's straight up diabolical! But when we put a dollar value on all the invisible work done worldwide, that stat explodes to $10.9 trillion per annum. Mathing the math here, that's more than the combined revenue of the fifty largest companies on 2019's Fortune Global 500 list, including Amazon, Apple, and Walmart.[2]

That part!!!

Understanding what invisible work is and why it's so insidious will be instrumental in saving your ass—trust. Invisible work is the silent killer of good marriages. Metaphorically speaking, it's the colon cancer of marital dysfunction. Ever so slowly and quietly, it will come for your butt. Here's how.

On a long enough timeline, as Wifey silently tackles the daily domestic grind of restocking groceries, doing laundry, and reloading the dishwasher, invariably, part of her fades away. The repetitive movements leech her psyche and she begins to ask herself, "Didn't I just clear the dishwasher?" "Am I the only one who notices that we're out of juice?" "Why am I always the one making up the bed?!" And while she's picking up the Legos for the umpteenth time this week or coordinating childcare, Husband (me) is loading dusty cheese doodles into his gullet and staring blankly into the void of some random screen. It dawns on her: She's alone.

Now, it's OK to get in your feelings about not knowing about invisible work or just how insidious and toxic it can be to a relationship. To some extent, we are all a product of what was modeled for us. For instance, I grew up in a home where my dad was almost always out of the house working. My mother was a college literature professor (where do you think I learned all my fancy-ass SAT words?), and my father was a gynecologist (nothing hilarious about that). As such, my dad pretty much stayed at the hospital delivering them babies, so when Father actually did come home and join us for dinner, he was dusted. After he finished his meal, he'd top off a glass of ice-cold Coke, retreat to the living room, and zone out to ESPN's early-nineties offerings, the blue light of the television washing over him like a fine mist.... See where I get it from?

Meanwhile, Mom was cleaning up the meal she just cooked. She did this day in and day out after teaching six or more college classes, picking up me and my siblings from our various schools, and shuttling us to and from our respective after-school activities. Though Mom's career wasn't life-or-death like Dad's, she definitely worked a full-ass day just like he did. And like many women of her era, she'd been liberated to the extent that she could join the workforce, but not to the extent that she was free from her domestic obligations. So, unlike my father, my mother had to hold down a job and a household, too.

See, my father had what Nobel Prize–winning economist Claudia Goldin would call a "greedy job."[3] That's not to say my father was greedy. He's perhaps the most generous person I know. By definition, greedy jobs are vocations that greedily demand one's time. More often than not, they are inflexible—that is, they prohibit one from spending time with one's partner, family, or friends—but they also (silver lining) pay more than "flexible" jobs like my mother's profession of teaching.

Of course, my dad wasn't delivering babies *every day* so there were times when he could have actually helped with the dishes or—gasp!—cooked, but for one reason or another, he didn't.

And, incidentally, my dad is a terrific cook! He taught my mother to cook. In pretty blatant violation of child labor laws, Dad grew up slanging hash in his family's late-night diner in Kalamazoo, Michigan. Ironically, the best cook in the house did not cook his family dinner unless my mom was completely out of commission. I remember because, like clockwork, my mom would catch a wicked flu right before Christmas when the concerting stresses of a concluding semester and the responsibilities of the holiday season conspired to wear her down. Miraculously, my dad would somehow muddle through without Mom, doing all that was necessary both in the house and at the hospital. All it took was a seasonal near collapse of my mother's immune system.

Of course, Dad's story isn't unique. Everyone I know has experienced this role reversal in one way or another. Either you've seen it play out as a child or you've been on the business end of a partner who is very unexpectedly out of commission.

But this fluke is so very revelatory. Of all my childhood memories, why do I cling to this *singular* flip in the routine?

Likely because Dad assuming Mom's regular household duties was such a departure from the unspoken lesson my parents were instilling. Mom does a whole day's worth of work like Dad, but then she's also expected to cook every meal, keep the house clean, attend to the children's schooling, health, grooming, activities, boo-boos, meltdowns, discipline, and more, all while caring for my grandmother, who was suffering through the ravages of Alzheimer's. My mother also did all the yardwork, which was not for the faint of heart, given that she did this in Texas in *August*! My brother and I would be right out there with her, pulling at nettles and trying to avoid the litany of fierce Texas fauna that seemed in an interminable race to kill us—scorpions, rattlers, and copperheads, oh my!

But where do we pick up these habits? They're usually not taught outright—no one sits you down and hands you a syllabus on gendered labor. Instead, these routines seep in through observation, absorbed like secondhand smoke.

Now, true, you could be reading this and saying to yourself #NotAllMen, but if you're reading these words, you or your partner or whoever tucked this little book under your pillow knows that there's a problem to solve. I can say from experience it's so easy to be blissfully unaware of the threat invisible work poses. And if this book was in fact slipped into your pocket by your person, you definitely need to lower your shields and take this in 'cause someone who loves you feels like you're not doing enough—and we need to figure out what "enough" is. The good news is that they're still wishing that you would.

So, how do we see invisible work? Great question. So glad I asked.

SPOTTING INVISIBLE WORK IN THESE STREETS

To be clear, neither of my parents ever said to me, "Women do this" and "Men do that" in our household. I just learned by watching, like in that awful antidrug ad from the eighties where a Dennis Franz type confronts his struggling teen about his drug use, and the kid blurts out, "I learned by watching you, Dad! I learned by watching you!" And don't get me wrong, my parents have been happily married for more than fifty years. They are deeply in love and somehow seem to grow closer with each passing anniversary (gross, I know). And my father was by no means lazy! He would often be on call for weeks on end, delivering babies at ungodly times of night—skirting death to usher in life. We were all used to him breaking out in the middle of a soccer game or a recital because someone, somewhere, was crowning!

But my point is he wasn't doing this *all* the time. On a day when he wasn't delivering yet another living miracle into this sputtering world, he just kind of switched off. I don't recall my father ever doing all that much on his days off but resting. So, in that sense, I was raised in a *super*-traditional household, wherein Dad was relieved of any household obligations, except for driving his kids to school on his way to the office because our schools and his office were in the same general direction. Yeah, my parents worked out a dynamic with its own internal logic, but it unwittingly set me up to believe that the breadwinner didn't have to pitch in around the house—an imprint that nearly drove my own marriage to the brink.

My parents' story is nothing new. If anything, it perfectly reflects the postwar, post–women's liberation movement nuclear-family dynamic. Instead of Dad being the sole breadwinner, now Mom is in the labor market too, *except* Dad works a super-demanding white-collar job that goes way longer than the nine-to-five blue-collar workday people quite literally died to secure. Meanwhile, Mom holds down a super-stressful gig herself but makes way less than Dad and *still* has to fulfill all the matronly duties she had before women's lib. So, in ways, my mom's generation made huge gains in the workforce, but they had to do this while also being saddled with the very same domestic responsibilities their moms dealt with.

And that's the thing—these dynamics didn't just shape my parents' marriage but also shaped my expectations. The idea that household responsibilities naturally fell to women wasn't just an unspoken rule in my home—it was baked into the very structure of how families operated for generations. But here's what I didn't fully grasp until much later: Although my dad's role was clear-cut, my mom's was endless.

That's where *invisible* comes in. It's all the behind-the-scenes labor that keeps a household running, and for the most part, it's gone unnoticed—especially by men. So let's break it down. Here's a big-butt list of tasks that are commonly regarded as invisible work. Study this. Take a pic of it and keep it handy. You may not have had anyone point these out for you. I don't know your life! And maybe you're already doing all these things; good for you, dude. Just bear in mind that this list isn't intended to make you feel like shit. Instead, it's to highlight the myriad things that go into running a home so that you don't have to fumble around like you're trying to find the bathroom light at three in the morning. They are things I definitely left to my partner to do solo until our marriage could no longer bear it. Feel free to list others in the comments if I've left them out. JK, this book doesn't have a comment section—but email me, really. We're all just trying to level up here, together, one overlooked chore at a time.

EXHAUSTIVE LIST OF TASKS COMPRISING INVISIBLE WORK AROUND THE HOME

Bedroom

Making up the bed
Cleaning bedroom
Changing sheets
Organizing drawers
Organizing closet
Hanging wet towels

Bathroom(s)

Restocking TP
Cleaning tub/shower
Replacing hygiene staples (toothpaste, shower gel, deodorant, Q-tips, floss, mouthwash, menstrual pads, tampons, etc.)
Replacing shower puff and/or luffa (side-eye if you only use your hands!)
Unclogging sink
Unclogging tub
Unclogging toilet
Cleaning bathmat
Cleaning towels
Hanging towels to dry
Mopping floor

Kitchen

Washing dishes
Emptying dishwasher (if you have one, that's a flex!)
Mopping floor
Cleaning stovetop
Cleaning oven
Putting away groceries
Keeping track of all groceries
Putting away dishes
Cooking
Replacing refrigerator air filter
Replacing refrigerator water filter
Taking out the garbage / recycling / compost
Cleaning microwave
Cleaning toaster
Cleaning coffeemaker
Cleaning blender
Sweeping kitchen floor

Living Room

Dusting
Changing light bulbs
Cleaning furniture
Deciding decor
Managing houseplants
Straightening all books, magazines, shoes, etc.
Vacuuming
Hospitality (aka homey vibes)

Pets

Walking
Grooming
Feeding
Training
Vet visits
Litter removal
Planning pet-sitting
Planning pet travel

Laundry

Washing clothes
Sorting clothes
Folding clothes
Ironing clothes
Taking clothes to and from the laundry room
Pretreating stains
Organizing laundry room
Clearing lint trap

Garage/Basement

Organizing
Deciding what to keep and what to toss
Bicycle maintenance
Car maintenance
Packing and unpacking the Christmas lights
Storing winter clothes
Storing summer clothes
Storing beach items
Storing gardening tools
Maintaining bad-weather gear: snow shovel, ice melt, sandbags, etc., depending on region
Safely storing hazardous materials

To quote the Notorious B.I.G., "If you don't know, now you know."[4]

This is a hell of a list, though I'm sure I've left out a lot. What can I say, though? I'm an oblivious dude who is game to learn, and I hope you are, too. Perhaps the most insidious aspect of invisible work is the amount of toxic resentment and silent suffering it creates within the burdened partner. It festers and boils unseen in the pressure cooker of dissonance until once-thriving bonds break down and sour. In a sense, invisible work is kinda like climate change. It's not good (some people even deny it's a thing), but we can totally do something about it, provided we are willing to put in the work.

Ugh, I know. That part.

Chapter 2

MASK ON

> If the cabin pressure changes, oxygen masks will drop from the overhead area. Secure your own mask first before helping others.
>
> —Literally every PSA before a flight ever

IF YOU'VE EVER FLOWN AND *NOT* SUCCUMBED TO THE GUSH OF pure oxygen pumped into the cabin preflight, you're no stranger to the oxygen mask instruction.

This announcement has always put me ill at ease. Why? Because the entire premise is anathema to who I am, or rather who I *think* I am. After watching way too many exhausting war movies and Sam Peckinpah westerns at my dad's knee, I tend to picture myself as the self-sacrificing type—generous and gallant—someone who puts the needs of others before his own. A latter-day Black knight, or "Knight of Color" (LOL) in a rugged time.

All that to say, this announcement always rubbed me the wrong way because, in my mind's eye, at least, I saw myself heroically helping someone else affix an oxygen mask to their face first, even if it meant my own asphyxiation. And if you'll indulge my unhinged fantasy this much more, I also thought that whomever I rescued would be the sole survivor of this very hypothetical tragedy. Then, long after this fortunate soul was miraculously plucked from the twisted wreckage, they would no doubt immortalize me with a life-size muscled-up bronze statue (that would someday be torn down for unforeseen political reasons), and children would sing songs in my honor every year on my birthday—in the coming era when alternate-side parking would inevitably be suspended, banks would naturally close, and flags would be lowered to half-staff by the area Cub Scout troop. What? *Ya gotta believe!*

For too long, I mistakenly believed that bold, heroic gestures would get me the glory and the girl, but as it turns out, life is not the movies. It's not even a limited series on a down-market streaming platform! What I've come to realize is that heroes are made and hearts are won via small-bore, everyday routines and tasks.

Honestly, that's the good news!

Turns out you don't have to save your family from bandits off the coast of Madagascar to finally earn your partner's respect. My totally wild take from a very unscientific yet profoundly effective field study of seventeen years of marriage to one person is that... [*checks notes*] if you want to save your relationship—if you want to save the *we*—ditch the self-sacrifice. I promise you it pays to go ten toes in on *me*, as long as we do some light dusting while we're at it. I have the receipts.

Now, this opinion may seem counterintuitive. After all, how can one improve a bond between two people by focusing on just one person? Well, take it from someone who has been through it—and stick with me here, because, as I will explain more fully, *Choreplay* is a practice of self-discipline. The point of choreplay is to shore up your relationship with yourself so that you bring a certain confidence to your relationship with your partner.

I have talked myself in circles with my person. I have therapized, date-nighted, stayed in, gotten away, journaled, and quite literally done *all the things* in an attempt to forge a deeper connection between us. None of these methods really worked. Then, out of sheer desperation, I kinda copied my old man.

When I was a kid, whenever my mom caught my dad sweeping up, doing the dishes, or folding laundry, et cetera, she'd crack a wry smile and joke that he was doing "choreplay." At the time, her bawdy bit went way over my head, thank God, but with time and too much life experience, I've come to understand what Mom meant. Dad was wooing Mom via household chores, and going out of his way to get caught in the act, too. Think what you will about his ruse, but that sly rogue has stayed married to Mom for nearly fifty-five years.

Thanks for the pearls, Dad. And thanks for the word, Mom. If you steal, steal from the best.

To be sure, I didn't intend to copy my dad. I didn't mean to stage myself cleaning with the hopes that Wife would catch me and give ye old pickle a tickle, and yet there was something there.

My dad was definitely onto something. There was something in there that could save any red-blooded male struggling to weather the unending pell-mell of toxic masculinity, the epidemic of male loneliness, or whatever else the manosphere was whining about this week, and I figured out what it was.

CHOREPLAY

So, what does choreplay involve, exactly? Great question. No notes!

To me, choreplay isn't *just* tidying up to *woo Boo*; it's a comprehensive self-discipline I totally backed into that successfully addressed imbalances within my relationship.

And here's what choreplay is not: It is not about splitting up duties evenly in order to clinically address this imbalance. 'Cause, as the old saying goes, "Sometimes what's equal isn't always fair. And sometimes what's fair isn't always equal."

Instead, choreplay is about heightening awareness and increasing participation in the upkeep of our respective bodies, minds, and homes. It's about remaining frosty and on the lookout for how we can actively address disorder within shared spaces by first addressing our own personal space. Put another way, choreplay is about, first and foremost, worrying about my side of the street. By concerning myself with *myself*, I was actually able to improve the conditions within my relationship writ large.

Thanks to choreplay, I went from thoughtless to aware, passive to proactive, lazy to lazy-but-seriously-working-on-it, and finally, unconcerned and unbothered to much more invested.

You get it.

Whereas once I was blind, now I'm not *totally* blind.

To get there, all it took was crawling out of my own butt.

NEVER AGAIN

I've had so many moments in my adult life that should have worked as moments of inflection, moments crying out to be *the* moment I started focusing on myself. My tendency, though, has been to ignore what the universe is trying to tell me. One such instance I will not soon forget.

We lay our scene way back in the days of flip phones, when my then girlfriend / now wife and I were moving closer and closer to the altar. Though I felt fortunate to be with my person, I was not comfortable. And my discomfort wasn't a function of anything my person was doing (she's a goddamn angel!). Rather, I was uncomfortable because of my own insecurities.

I believed deeply that my partner was out of my league and that one morning, she would wake up, realize this, and rightly leave my loser ass. Yes, up until *literally* about two years ago this was how I operated in my now twenty-plus-year relationship. I even normalized this dysfunction and told myself this was just part of being married to a woman as intelligent and beautiful as my wife. This was the price I needed to pay, I thought.

My MO from day one of our relationship was to sacrifice my own happiness and peace of mind for hers. I didn't matter. My thinking was that if my partner could see the sacrifices great and small that I made for her daily, ultimately, I would somehow be rewarded every time I acquiesced to go to the movie *she* wanted to go to or stay home on a picture-perfect Saturday night as *she* wanted. I dreamed of somehow amassing imaginary points for always agreeing to vacation wherever *she* wanted. I thought that my then girlfriend / now wife was silently cataloging these selfless acts.

As it turns out, she was not.

I also mistook not speaking my feelings or wants as somehow *virtuous*. Yeah, I really had my head up my ass....

Anyway, on this one particular day, I was supposed to catch a flight up to Portland, Maine, from our home in New York City. My wife was already in Maine, and I had hung back for a couple of days because of work. I recall that the flight wasn't early—around ten in the morning or so.

Now, let me just stop on a dime to tell you that I am "an Old." I am Gen X, millennial rising. All that to say, I called a cab. Yes! There was a time when one actually *called* jitney cabs rather than letting your thumbs do the talking. Anyhoo, the cab finally comes, and I run out of my apartment building to tell the cabbie that I just need to grab my bag and lock up, but when I turn around to grab said possessions and lock said doors, I realize that I've walked out of my apartment without my keys.

Oh, and in case you're wondering, the door to my apartment shut and locked automatically and my then girlfriend / future wife was in Maine, so yes, I was fucked—proper fucked.

What did I do? Rather than call future wife to tell her that I beefed it and couldn't make the flight because I didn't have my stuff, I kept that part to myself and raced to make the flight... with zero luggage. *Who does that?*

Answer: this idiot.

I locked myself out of my apartment, which is vexing AF. But rather than giving myself a moment to regroup, be realistic, and find a long-term solution, I sucked it up.

I made the flight to Maine, where I immediately dove into an outdoor supply store and got myself a fleece, which I still own to this day. In part, I think I've held on to it as long as I have because it serves as some kind of grim reminder of how I struggle to look out for myself. But even after I'd made it to Portland, my saga wasn't over. I had to take an hourlong ferry to a tiny island in the bay where I finally met up with my person.

On the pier of this tiny scenic speck in Casco Bay, my wife asked where my things were. I told her what happened, and her face just dropped. I thought that she would be jazzed that I had forsaken myself to make the flight and get to her.

Incorrect.

Here's what I should have done. I should have called a locksmith and taken a later flight. Shit happens. If the roles were reversed, she would have reset. There's literally zero chance Wife would have flown to the Frozen North with no clothes and no toothbrush. Are you serious?! Meanwhile, I was flying with zero suitcases but a whole lotta baggage.

Why couldn't I offer myself grace at that moment rather than taking off to the airport with little more than the clothes I was wearing? The looks I got from airport security personnel when I told them that I didn't have any luggage on a *one-way* flight was really not worth it.

And this story sticks with me because it feels like the moment was trying desperately to teach me something—and I willfully ignored the lesson.

SUCK IT UP

When I was a kid, if I got banged up, bruised, or ever so lightly strafed/maimed in the presence of my father, he'd say, "Suck it up, Big Fella. Suck it up."

To an extent, I agree with my father. Not everything in life is going to break your way, so you'd better make peace with it. All of us are going to experience pain in one form or another. But my father and I grew up in different eras and in totally different situations.

The "suck it up" mentality was necessary to my father's survival. My father was born rich, then lost everything. His father abandoned the family, and my father became the man of the house at ten years old. Strapped with the stress of raising three young children in 1950s America, my grandmother soon suffered a debilitating stroke that left her an invalid. As a boy, my dad took up work at a late-night greasy spoon, slinging hash and serving drunken nighthawks in his hometown of Kalamazoo. He worked odd jobs throughout his boyhood and adolescence, including but not limited to working at a Detroit Pontiac auto plant where molten lead somehow fell from the assembly line, burned through his work boot, and scorched his foot.

The guy survived wretched, grinding poverty and somehow got himself into medical school, and through sheer will and my mother's love and support, he became a successful doctor. Given all that, it stands to reason, then, that my dad would advise me time and again to deal with hardship the way he did—by just sucking it up. Dad didn't have the opportunity to reset or to self-soothe. As someone negotiating poverty, he didn't have the time.

Survival doesn't permit a whole lot of emotional check-ins and meditative moments. It demands that you put one foot in front of the other; keep it moving, or else.

Problem is, I adopted my dad's survival tactics and applied them in places where I was not "surviving." The results were predictably overwrought and often disproportionate to whatever mild setback I was facing.

For a long time, my primary means of meeting a problem was to fall on my own sword, which is well and good if the sky itself is falling, but not if you simply lock yourself out of your house and are, in so doing, *maybe* a little waylaid on your journey to your future in-laws' summer place on a picturesque island in Maine. My tendency to go into self-sacrifice mode at the drop of a hat cost me my self-respect. I didn't know how to look out for myself. I wanted to be a martyr so badly that I was spoiling for any opportunity to be one.

My dad's dad was a gangster, a crook, and a wife-beater who brought pain and misery to my father and his family. To survive this trauma, my dad learned to suck it up and never complain. I inherited that lesson like gospel. Maybe you did too—maybe you've spent years swallowing frustration, showing up big in obvious ways, while the quieter, daily labor—emotional labor, household labor, the constant mental tabs—was left to your partner, unnoticed. You tell yourself you're pulling your weight, but something's off.

I see now that I was a grand-gesture, self-sacrificing kind of guy to make up for all the things I left my wife to shoulder it all in silence.

HAPPY WIFE, HAPPY LIFE?

"Happy wife, happy life" is an adage of many a partner who has somehow muddled through the institution of marriage. It's cute, and it rhymes, and I've used it countless times to answer the question "What's your secret to a long and healthy marriage?" What this twee, little saying belies is how much the speaker is likely just placating their partner. That was definitely the case for me.

Truth is, my "yes, dear" routine was turning me more salty and resentful by the day. *Where was my spine? Where was Jordan in all this?* To me, Wife's happiness came at the expense of my own.

For years, I felt that if I was not happy but Wife was, then who was I to say anything, right? "Suck it up, son." I'd hear Dad's words ringing in my ears. "Walk it off, Big Fella," he'd say. Turns out, there's a limit to how much we all can suck it up, walk it off, or otherwise ignore our own feelings. On a long enough timeline, to quote Springsteen, you have to "cut it loose or let it drag you down."[1]

In this instance, the "it" was my habit of never putting my oxygen mask on first. I had to learn to do that before it did me and my marriage in. I had to find a way to want to pick up after myself, to eat right, to sleep right, to give helpful notes, to take criticism without losing it, and even to change my shopping habits and switch to bulk to save my own time and mind. And I had to find a way to do it not just for the sake of my partner but also for my own sake.

In this book, we are going to learn that taking care of yourself genuinely benefits you *and* your partner. For me, the change did not come all at once. It was gradual. It took time to actually believe in myself and my own self-worth. It took dedication, discipline, effort, and faith to show up for me—but when I did, when my sense of self finally came online at the tender age of forty-six (just a tween, really), I felt like I'd elevated myself. In so doing, I elevated my relationships, too.

I took up space.

I kept up my end more often, and the weight of being, the everyday domestic grind, seemed at least negotiable.

I despaired less. I planned more.

I got in the fight.

Relationships are not for the timid—full stop. They will grind you. They will test you and put you through your paces. The question is: Are you equal to the challenge?

Yes, my guy, you are.

Like a tectonic shift, something finally gave inside me, and what was once static finally got rolling.

Through the routines I will share with you, I have come to life for the first time in years. Laundry, dishes, and straightening are no longer as daunting as they once were. They have been reduced and reframed. There is time. They are no longer the source of domestic strife that they once were, namely, because they have been swept up into a larger sea change. 'Cause what is picking up after others if I'm already in the habit of picking up after myself?

Chores don't need divvying up when you change your nature and emotionally move out of your mom's house. Your partner is not your mother-substitute or your maid. They are your partner. And sure, acts of service have long been recognized as one of the love languages, but here's where choreplay distinguishes itself from a love language. To me, choreplay begins not with overtures designed to please one's partner but, instead, as you will come to see, with the focus on pleasing ourselves.

Choreplay is about self-possession and a dab or two of healthy self-concern. It's about removing yourself from your partner's plate of concerns, but not by diminishing yourself—but instead by spreading your wings, taking up space, and living for yourself in ways big and small.

I had to learn that the hard way, but lucky for me, I learned in time. And if you reach the end of this tiny-ass book, you will too.

OKAY, DEAREST READER, YOU'VE ASCENDED A FLOOR AND didn't get your toes mangled in the teeth of the escalator on the way up, so, bravo! Here's what we're serving up on Level One.

This stage is all about the reset. We're going to talk about the temporarily painful art of finding time in your busy life to address what may well be holding you back. Then we are going to discuss carving out more space to flex our mindfulness muscles, and finally we'll address the fact that none of us are getting any younger no matter how much we moisturize—something my crow's feet, gray hairs, and love handles tell me every day.

Chapter 3

ASSESS YOUR MESS

The Length, Width, and Depth of the Shaft

There are known knowns; there are things we know we know. We also know there are known unknowns; that is to say we know there are some things we do not know. But there are also unknown unknowns—the ones we don't know we don't know.

—Donald Rumsfeld[1]

AFTER MANY YEARS TOGETHER—MOST PRETTY GREAT—MY marriage of thirteen years was in trouble. The problem was that I was running out of time, like *I'm-cramming-for-tomorrow's-Louisiana-State-Bar-exam-but-haven't-managed-to-open-the-dusty-ass-Napoleonic-Code-textbook-until-now* level of running out of time. Like John McClane in *Die Hard* "Do I cut the red wire or the blue wire?" level of running out of time! But how in Beyoncé's world had we gotten here?

The answer wasn't complicated. Allow me to rewind the clock.

When I met my wife, I was a young copywriter on Madison Avenue. I had an apartment in Greenwich Village and a vintage 1970s BMW coupe—stick shift with race car handling (yes, I was once cool) (yes, there's a theme in this book). But then I gave all that up to pursue my comedy dreams, which sent me into an exhausting tumult of ups and downs, false highs, rejections, and crushing periods of depression—aka Life in the Arts. If you didn't know, stand-up comedy is among the more treacherous and psychologically fraught mediums (besides assistant rodeo clown, obviously), but at least the drinks are free (and I'm not sure you can say the same for rodeo clowns).

Given all that, I am considered a *relatively* successful comic. I've written for multiple seasons of late-night TV (two), starred in short-lived TV series (two), cohosted a successful podcast, and so much more. But for all the occasional glitz and minimal glamour, let me tell you there are vast gulfs and periods when the work will not come... at all, where for one reason or another (labor strikes, labor strikes, and oh yeah, more labor strikes)—or simply hard luck—I cannot get a gig. These times seem to stretch on like the line for the shitters at Yankee Stadium. They exact a heavy toll on my self-worth and confidence and send me into an existential tailspin so deep I question/regret ever wanting to make people laugh in the first place. Awful, I know, but we haven't even gotten to the worst part yet! (And, yes, there's a worse part, because there's a handy trapdoor at the bottom of this pit that allows you to sink even lower.)

It's the loneliness that comes from being home and acutely unemployed while the world rushes by you, people getting on with their lives as you wait for some glimmer on the horizon, some dim hope or prospect. The agony of it all can be so total that you feel hopelessly subsumed by self-loathing and self-pity. Let's just say comedy ain't for the weak. Now, if I *weren't* married and stuck in my home amid my own filth and detritus, that would be fine and dandy, but I have a person, and these days I have kids, and swanning about like Black Hamlet is not going to cut it.

When I moved in with my soon-to-be fiancée / now wife, I was confronted with the harsh reality of living with another person, particularly a tidy one. To be clear, I'd had a roommate when I first moved to New York, but in that scenario, I was the clean one (yikes!), which meant I cleaned our dank-ass windowless bathroom once or twice a year and then washed the dishes after that one time I saw a fidgety mouse scurry out of the drain and nestle into my favorite coffee cup. So, obviously, living with someone as fastidious and orderly as my then girlfriend / soon-to-be fiancée / now wife was somewhat of a blindside to my inner sloth.

For the record, Wifey is scary organized. She graduated cum laude from Smith College (not level easy shit), and while

I was farting my way through my comedy career, Wife was helping to create a specialized high school in her hometown of Brooklyn. My highly motivated, meticulous, and brilliant wife happens to be a paragon of order and routine. So, living with a Jabba the Hutt–esque slob like *moi* would present a few challenges.

First off, after I moved in, she seemed to want to go grocery shopping basically *every* weekend (what the fuck was that about?!). She also expected us to do our laundry every week, cook meals, *and* eat together (not normal!). And because I remained in the house so much—*so much*!—as a broke-ass, struggling entertainer, it fell on me to make sure that our apartment was tidy, that the trash was sorted, and that the bed was made. It wasn't much to ask, given that I was home all day, and yet it was a struggle. I recall wondering aloud as to why the apartment needed cleaning all the time. As a couple, we do not host. We lived in deepest Brooklyn, and we could be incredibly antisocial homebodies. *Who were we cleaning up for here?!* Back then, I barely cleaned, rarely cooked, woke up around eleven, and left piles of my clothes around like massive sartorial nests. It's safe to say that, if I didn't live with my wife, my apartment would have been a contender for that show *Hoarders*.

Resentment took hold, and I soon began to associate tidying with failure. As in, because I couldn't get steady work, I was a failure relegated to domestic tasks, waiting for the breadwinner to return home at the close of a long day, at which point I would have her vodka gimlet and slippers waiting. At the time, that felt shameful and like one more sign that I hadn't made it at all. What's more, being in our apartment definitely did a number on my mental health. Did I really come all the way to New York to dust and straighten? To walk the dog and do the cooking? The daily repetition of it all ate away at my weakling's ego. Then things really came to a head the year I basically made *zero dollars whatsoever.* At the risk of hyperbole, it felt like Jean-Claude Van Damme boot-kicked me in the tender ball sack of my soul.

With tears streaming down my face on our tiny Wayfair couch, I promised Wife that, if things didn't turn around by year's end, I would quit entertainment and try something new despite having no actual job skills to speak of. However, I couldn't have picked a worse year to make this promise. It was 2009, and the economy writ large was still "recovering" (code for the rich getting richer and the poors doing what the poors will do) from the 2008 housing crisis, and on top of that, Hollywood was in the midst of a writers' strike (our major output, it would seem!).

All that to say, 2009 (for me, at least) was a professional wasteland—no work and no prospects—cue the blues guitar! Then after months of trying and on the eve of my promised career pivot, by sheer dumbass luck, I landed a teensy role in a TV ad for Crestor heart meds that basically played *everywhere* for literal *years*. But in so doing, it threw my ass a serious lifeline. Checks streamed into my mailbox—thanks, Daddy Big Pharma! Suddenly, I could help pay the rent. I could pick up the bill at dinner or buy gifts on holidays. We could even go on trips!

Logically, I know full well that money should have no bearing on my feelings of self-worth. Still, we live in a capitalist society where, whether we believe it or not, we have all bought into the system to one extent or another, so don't @ me for admitting my checking account balance contributed to my mood. Like a lot of people, when my balance is up, I'm up, and when it's down . . . say less.

Of course, in retrospect, I see getting that heart pill ad as more a bullet dodged than a lesson learned. A few years after my heart attack medicine TV ad success, I began to get more breaks. It took a long-ass time, but I started to build a career, and soon, I became so busy with work that I was hardly home—far from the pain and the shame I associated with domestic duties. I mean, who cares if my clothes are in gross piles on the floor and I never put my dishes away if I'm on sets with celebrities and getting paid TV money, *amiright, ladies?!* And so it went.

I dealt with my issues surrounding sharing the load with my wife by hiding behind my blossoming comedy career. Success in comedy equated to a huge middle finger to housework and, by extension, my marriage. *Want me to take out the trash?* Sorry, I'm needed on set! *Need me at that parent–teacher conference?* Sorry, I'm needed on set! *Need me to soothe my kids as they navigate this wasteland we call the modern world?* I'm sorry, but what part of "They need me on set" are you not understanding exactly? And remember what had been modeled for me as a kid: The man didn't do housework. He provided.

Doing housework of any kind was anathema. It did not compute. And the better I did in my career, the less I did around the house until, eventually, my only role was that of subsidizer.

Then, COVID-19 struck. I was back at home and out of work; it was basically 2009 all over again. Except now I had two wonderful children and a cute-ass cockapoo, which, if you don't know, is a high-end mix between a poodle and a cocker spaniel and mercifully not called a "poocockie," which in my mind is just a neighborhood away from the notorious "bukaki!"... Again, I digress.

Much had changed since my 2009 career low *except* my unaddressed issues surrounding housework. If anything, I was somehow even more loath to pitch in than before.

Once again, I could feel the long-dormant thorns of anxiety surrounding housework beginning to dig deep into my psyche. But there would be no juicy project or time-intensive Hollywood gig to give me cover from my responsibilities this time. Of course, the all-too-sudden way work stopped didn't do me any favors, but if I had made even the slightest effort to integrate myself more fully into the rhythms of our household, perhaps the next part could have been avoided.

After months of emotional flailing and cringy self-pity, my marriage drifted like a rudderless barge into the shoals of a full-on crisis, and what I was doing (or rather, what I wasn't doing) was hurting the family unit. The time and energy I spent sulking and brooding in my profound self-absorption left me disinterested and supremely disinclined to do much of anything, much less help around the house. That long-buried, unconfronted belief that housework was the province of losers unable to provide anything material was boiling over, and my head was most decidedly up my ass.

I couldn't have chosen a worse time to spiral into my Paperless Post pity party for one, though. Because after years of not being around much, my family had more or less gotten along without me. They had rhythms and routines that did not include me, and now that I was home, it felt super awkward, like I was the dude who brought the kazoo to the rap battle.

I was solely to blame for rendering myself redundant and unnecessary to the daily goings-on in my home. Sure, I was in the house, but at the risk of sounding trite, I was not in the home. I think it was the closest I've ever come to being a ghost without the whole being dead part. But unlike other ghosts who always seem to be getting hunted, zero people noticed me. I was an ineffective, sometimes friendly ghost.

Real talk, I might as well not have been there at all. I wasn't helping out with the kids. I wasn't cooking. I wasn't cleaning. My wife pretty much had to remind me to do everything, which must have been exhausting.

As a comedian, I don't pat myself on the back often (depending on who you ask, of course). I usually scoff at compliments and ignore glowing praise (hello, imposter syndrome!).

But I will give myself this much: I have a keen knack for reading a room and picking up on vibes, and suffice it to say, the vibes in my home at the time were fraught AF. My antennae were receiving serious torrents of unspoken consternation and vexation. The source was Wife. She was pretty much done with my antics. Change was definitely in the wind. It was only a matter of time. While I was spiraling, Wifey kept waxing romantically about her freshly divorced friends, finally liberated from their boorish, slothful mates.

I'd have been a fool not to pick up on the not-so-subtle messages, and if you are hearing the same, you'd be too. For instance, if any books by Esther Perel suddenly appear on her nightstand, your ass is pretty much cooked! And that's what it was for me—the unheralded arrival of relationship expert Esther Perel's content. Trust. I say this player to player and pimp to pimp (calm down, this is a line from *Training Day*): If she's left anything of Perel's oeuvre out for you to see, and she's not studying to be someone's therapist, it has to be a subtle warning shot. The call is coming from inside the house! Time to course correct whatever you're doing, 'cause it ain't working.

I wish I could tell you that after I noticed Wifey's new reading materials, we both sat down as mature adults on our L-shaped couch, looked lovingly into each other's souls, and patiently hashed out how *we* could dig out of this, but that's not what happened. When you've been married so long that you have to look at each other to recall how you met, and you've already had nearly every stripe of every relationship conversation you're going to have, there is precious little left that your partner can give to improve the state of the union. Simply put, sometimes it's on you.

My wife had done all the convincing, coaxing, and cajoling she was going to do with me. She was tired of having to wake me up in the morning (I didn't even set an alarm) and asking me to take the kids to school and reminding me to take out the trash. If we were going to remain together, it would require change on my part, not hers. Either I was going to do the now-visible work, or I was going to become a fun, every-other-weekend dad with a beer gut and witty graphic tees. The choice was mine, really.

I didn't want to become the latter, a predictable midlife trope, so I regrouped and resolved to grow the fuck up (again, depending on who you ask). The only trouble is that, once you make a pact with yourself to, like, *grow*, pulling it off becomes the slog. You need a plan (ick). You need discipline (no thanks). But above all, you need something else that always seems in short supply: time enough to figure it the fuck out!

I had precious few hours to clear my head between family, trying to find work, and all the other spam life threw my way. But I did have one thing going for me. For better or worse, I am very good at adapting relatively quickly. So quickly that it scares me sometimes (and, yes, I am in therapy, thank you so much!). Yet I'm also too good at holding on to habits that don't serve me—aren't we all?

What am I getting at, you say?

This is the part of the book where I ask you to give something up. Not like a *Thanos-dashing-his-greenish-adoptive-daughter-on-the-rocks-to-attain-the-brown-Infinity-Stone* level of sacrifice—but this ask might hurt a bit. Nothing crazy. If I had to assess the pain level, I would say it ranks at inadvertently pulling a couple of chest hairs out by the root with double-sided tape or smashing your pinky toe while farting around in the kitchen for a late-night munchie. We're talking about a level of pain that's more in the league of lightweight maiming, but not mortal wounding—that kind of energy. And now that I've managed your expectations, please know that what I am presenting you ain't a cure-all. It's a tourniquet, 'cause, emotionally speaking, your femoral artery is severed and gushing apace. It'll solve the problem so we can then *solve the problem.*

This hack gave me time to figure out my next move. There's a good chance it will work for you too.

IT'S TIME TO HANG UP THE JERSEY OR YOUR SOCCER CLEATS OR YOUR MMA GLOVES OR CONTROLLER OR WHATEVER FORM OF GEAR FITS HERE

When things went south in my relationship, I knew if I was going to have any chance of course correcting, I needed a bit of daylight to triage. Lucky for me, I am a super-casual Dallas Cowboys fan—hold for jeers. And I can honestly say the ne'er-do-well Dallas Cowboys and their losing ways helped me get my life back.

Listen, I'm from Dallas, so I grew up obsessed with "The Boys." Emmitt Smith, Michael Irvin, Troy Aikman, and Jay Novacek were my heroes, and I was fortunate enough to watch this mythic team march Sunday after glorious Sunday to three Super Bowl titles in the 1990s. It was a joyous time to be a citizen of Cowboys Nation. In Texas, football is religion, and Cowboys Football was bigger than God herself. But what's bigger than God, right? (Wi-Fi...?)

Suffice it to say that at least during the regular season, NFL football upstaged the sweet Baby Jesus himself. Ministers across the state knew that there was a lot in the race for their congregation's soul, especially the Dallas Cowboys. I can recall many a hot Texas Sunday when the minister would pause briefly from holding forth about eternal damnation to roast all the Cowboys fans who were hoping for him to just kind of wrap up his sermon so we could get home in time to change out of our stuffy church clothes into our jeans and T-shirts for kickoff.

"Now I know many of you are eager to get home and watch the Dallas Cowboys play on TV," he'd say with a wry smile. *How did the preacher know what I was thinking?!* Had the Baby Jesus told him?! No disrespect to Jehovah, turning water into wine and feeding the five thousand with a loaf and a half of bread are great and all, but the Dallas crew were modern-day warrior-poets out there performing IRL miracles that made me say the Lord's name in vain on the regular!

After that glorious gilded age, though, the Cowboys didn't make another Super Bowl appearance until... ever. Why is anyone's guess, really. Whatever the cause of the Cowboys' slow, twenty-plus-year implosion, I dutifully continued to watch roster after ill-fated roster try and *flail* through the sine curves of winning seasons and meh seasons, and categorically apocryphal ones, too. And though I always lived in hope that my Boys would someday return to their former glory (Cowboys Nation always lives in hope), I started to wonder if the three or more hours I spent every Sunday for sixteen (now seventeen) weeks of the year was really worth all the grief. Each game had its share of thrills and fun, and who doesn't love a new potentially controversial beer ad or a Taco Bell commercial featuring the scruffy charms of Pete Davidson as he promotes newly reconfigured maize, meat, and cheese offerings?

But, at a certain point, a Cowboys game became little more than something on in the background of my home, a handy excuse to veg out on the Lord's Day. I definitely wasn't paying as much attention as I once did. But then there was so much turnover and tumult on the roster season to season that you would have thought Elon Musk had bought the franchise. Beyond the Pro Bowlers, I couldn't name you a single starter—defensive or offensive—even if it meant the debt ceiling or Great Pacific Garbage Patch would magically cease to exist.

But for some reason I faithfully executed my duties as a citizen of Cowboys Nation. I preserved, protected, and defended America's team from any and all detractors and haters at bars, BBQs, get-togethers, shindigs, soirees, Super Bowl parties, christenings, bar and bat mitzvahs, Easter egg rolls, log rolls, charity 5Ks, and bakes or Irish wakes. If anyone was going to beat up on the Cowboys, it was gonna be me! In case it isn't clear by this point, cognitive dissonance and shared delusion are major hallmarks of Cowboys Nation ('cause it's pretty much a cult).

Let's do the math. Remember, we came here because we don't have time for invisible work, right? But viewing a single season of Cowboys games meant that, for a *minimum* of forty-eight hours (16 games × 3 hours per game = 48 hours) per season, I was adhered to my couch. That's a whole two consecutive days of me creating cushion crevasses in dank-ass sweats and churning out nacho farts—at minimum.

I share this because any football fan worth their salt is likely doing the same—watching their team's games from start to finish week in and week out, whether on a couch or at a bar, wherever. If I was really going in, I would watch football from 1:00 p.m. (when the games tend to begin on the East Coast) until 11:00 p.m., when Sunday night football finally and sadly signed off. Sunday alone could mean a potential ten-hour TV viewing jag! Yikes! And don't get me started on Monday night and Thursday night football. Everyone has their hobbies and their needed rest or escape, but there comes a point when we need to be honest with ourselves and really consider how much time our distractions are costing us. I mean, when you follow the punter's dog on IG, you've probably watched enough.

It did help that NFL has become so fraught. Between the horrors of CTE—chronic traumatic encephalopathy, which degenerates brains—and the disgusting fallout surrounding Colin Kaepernick's nonviolent protest against the ills and existential threat posed by any cop who sucks at their job, not to mention the Cowboys continuing to break my heart, I realized that sooner or later I was going to have to get out of this very toxic, one-sided relationship. And with my back very much against the wall in my very real, not parasocial relationship, I decided (gulp!) to break up with the Cowboys.

It was hard, because that team was one of my few remaining connections to Texas. It was yet another part of who I was. But, in reality, it's also fair to say I broke up with the Cowboys as much as the Cowboys broke up with me. The soul-crushing Dez Bryant noncatch against the Green Bay Packers in the 2014 wildcard game was a bit too much for my spirit or, as we say below the Mason-Dixon, "ma spurt."

But I realized what was required was not a shift in my identity but more so a shift in my patterns. And, look, you might not even be into watching sports (weird but OK). Gaming or even watching gamers game could be your thing, but we all have our own wastes of time that we *think* are restful, but they're really just wastes of time.

Bottom line, I couldn't just keep being a subfunctioning lump on the couch who grudgingly did his wife's bidding in between commercial breaks or during the Fox NFL halftime show (sorry, Jimmy, Terry, Howie, and Curt). It wasn't enough. I couldn't let myself get absorbed into yet another game as my marriage unraveled. It might sound kinda random and dumb, I know, but it's like rearranging deck chairs on the *Titanic*—keeping myself busy with meaningless tasks while the real problem loomed larger beneath the surface.

When I stopped watching football, I could not believe how much time I suddenly had! Holy shit! I was swimming in it—doing backstrokes even! Newly free from my oceans of time-consuming Monday, Thursday, and Sunday football watching, I could actually dedicate energy to getting my shit together. (And believe me, I move very slowly and require literally *all* the time I can get, so this was huge for me.)

I got plugged into family life. I could do weekend errands and not feel rushed and, moreover, resentful. I had time to go for a run or to take my kids out for a fun/low-stakes adventure while my wife did whatever she wanted. I could go on a country drive or take a long Sunday brunch—*and* occasionally check my phone for the scores and standings. I even found time to finish that book that had been eluding me, too. Imagine that!

And after getting somewhat comfortable with this new scheme, I was able to finally assess my mess and what role I was playing in my own dysfunction. Now, I'm not advocating that you full-on cold-turkey quit watching football as I did, or any of your favorite sports for that matter (actually, I literally am), but what I mean is that you should consider the cost-benefit to your marriage of mindless distractions. I mean, sorry to yuck anyone's yum out here, but when we watch professional sports, it's reasonable to say we are watching multimillionaires and, in some cases, billionaires—especially if you're watching men's sports—play games. Who does that serve, exactly? No disrespect to these athletes, but I've given you all enough of my time and money.

I think God (Oprah) put it best when he (she? Idk) said in 1 Corinthians 13:11, "When I was a child, I spake as a child, I understood as a child, I thought as a child: but when I became a man, I put away childish *thangs*."[2] And are you really going to argue with Yahweh? OK, fine, maybe you don't believe in God (or maybe you wish he'd just believe in himself for once?).

Point is, my take on all this was summed up by a very unlikely source. Comedian, critic, and legendary New York grump Fran Lebowitz threw down a fire take for anyone questioning their own toxic addiction to sports during a back-and-forth with another legendary New York grump and long-suffering Knicks fan, Spike Lee, in her 2021 docuseries *Pretend It's a City*:[3]

Spike Lee: So why do you hate sports?

Fran Lebowitz: You see these people in the streets. They're screaming, "We won! We won!" and I'm always thinking, "Who's we?" They won, and you lay on the sofa drinking beer.

Spike Lee: But that's the great thing about sports. You identify with the team.

Fran Lebowitz: Yeah, which is a business. You never see people in the street going, "Yay! Coke won! Pepsi lost!" How they got you to do this, I'd like to know that.

Speak on it, Fran! What did I really owe the Cowboys? No doubt, they gave me some wonderful memories: Sunday afternoons in front of the TV with my brother and my dad, Monday night nail-biters, and Super Bowl parties where everyone whooped and jeered Dallas to immortality! But that was a looooong time ago, FanDuel doesn't own me, and it's not like the kids are sitting there making memories of their own. And these millionaires truly are not out here paying my bills, despite my best efforts to hit up Cowboys owner Jerry Jones via Cash App (jokes).

Again, I'm not saying you should stop watching sports altogether. It is among the only things keeping live TV afloat right now (that and *The Golden Bachelor*), and I am a sentimental fool. But what I am saying is that a flotilla of positives came my way when I let go of watching *so much* goddamn football and basketball, and honestly tennis too. I am not trying to recruit anyone to this lifestyle like I'm out here in multilevel marketing, but what I am saying is that watching less sports helped me find the time to figure my life out.

At some point, anyone trying to make a productive life change has to let go of what really isn't serving them. That's really the lesson here. For me, that meant cutting out sports, but then everyone's journey is different. I'm not perfect, y'all. I still read little articles about the Cowboys here or there, or stalk them on Instagram to see who they're dating and if they let themselves go or not. If they mention me, please let me know... or don't. It's all too painful!

Again, if you're reading this book, it's very likely that either you or your partner feels that something's got to give (probably sooner than later). Doesn't seem fair, does it? *Why should we have to give something up? Why should we have to change?* Well, there's a mantra I keep handier than a pocket pack of Kleenex in April for moments like these, and you've heard it already. "Sometimes what's fair isn't always equal. And sometimes what's equal isn't always fair." I am begging you to take this in and not fling the book into the corner upon reading, but rather appreciate the yin-yang woo-woo symmetry therein.

Proper sacrifice is a searing and difficult thought to absorb. It's also a very hard truth to accept, but sometimes creating an equitable dynamic requires cutting something loose, 'cause *something* ain't working.

Dear reader, I don't know how you were raised, or how the world treats you, but personally I was never promised "fair."

Unless you're cutting the chocolate chip cookie with a guided laser, someone will always get the bigger half. My advice is to keep a healthy sense of perspective. Such is the give-and-take, symbiotic nature of any healthy relationship. Maybe at the outset of your relationship it wasn't like this. Maybe vegging on the couch or day drinking with the crew was permissible, cute even. But that was of a time and times change. What we do in our twenties just hits differently in our thirties and forties. That is to say, forty-and-older me parked in front of the widescreen with gray stubble and matching gray sweats dappled with salsa stains is somehow less appealing than my twenty-something version of the same. Is that fair? Well, I've heard of more just things, but that's beside the point. The point is that relationships are not static. They are living and ever evolving. They require regular adjustment—sometimes micro, sometimes macro.

For me, that meant scrapping football. Now, maybe you don't want to quit football whole hog like I did. Maybe you're reading this and getting the feeling that the medicine is somehow worse than the cure. And it is true, no two relationships are the same. But you're here to help yourself with this book, so... if we aren't in the same boat, my guy, we are definitely in the same storm.

The truth is, we all need to at least consider budging on some of our habits and guilty pleasures, 'cause inertia is not our friend here. So, spotlight's on you now. It's your turn to do a quick diagnostic of your own.

Answer the following questions honestly, 'cause seriously, there are only two, and no one will ever hear what you think on this. The key here is just to catalog your behavior. Once you're aware, acting on that knowledge is up to you.

Also, fucking act on that knowledge!

How many hours a week do you engage in the following activities?

Watching sports
Playing in fantasy leagues
Gaming
Gambling
Late-night binge-watching
Reading graphic novels
Listening to podcasts
Flipping through YouTube
Scrolling Instagram
TikTok
Reddit boards
Porn
Larping (feels like I shoulda ended with porn, right?)

How can you keep these fun distractions and also improve your marriage?

You can't have your cake (read: porn) and keep your marriage, too. Everything comes with a price, but if I can put down the Cowboys and all their tiresome / dramatic / chaotic AF shenanigans, I have every confidence in you to do the same. Just tell yourself, if you watch, your team will lose. Thank me later!

JUST THE TIPS, PLEASE

- Taking a step back to assess what role YOU play in your relationship's dysfunction is critical.
- Find ways to give your partner more of your time and attention, even if it means cutting out beloved distractions.
- Habits that were cute in our twenties don't always age well.

Chapter 4

EXECUTIVE FUNCTION

What's Your Function?

As ever, Watson, you see, but you do not observe.

—Sherlock Holmes, in
Sir Arthur Conan Doyle's
"A Scandal in Bohemia"

QUICK STORY THAT HAS NOTHING/EVERYTHING TO DO WITH MY relationship.

My sister gets offended whenever I offer her chocolate.

Why? Because she hates things that are unassailably good and delicious?

Maybe.

But in this case, my sister is dreadfully allergic to chocolate. It gives her the bubble guts something terrible! Love ya, sis!

She has reminded me of this repeatedly, and yet my forgetful ass still keeps offering her bowl after frozen bowl of B&J's chocolate ice cream with damn delectable bits of fudge brownie shoved all up in it for an extra dollop of "Thank you, sir, may I have another!"

I reflexively offer up the sweet brown stuff like she didn't already say the part about how if she's served chocolate it best come with a side of EpiPen and a dash of Benadryl. My sister, who is otherwise a very sweet and lovely individual, readily gets in her feelings whenever I do this. Can you blame her? I'm her brother. It's reasonable to assume that I should retain some key details about her, no? Today, I can't imagine how irksome it must have been for her to keep explaining her allergies to me time and time again, and then have none of them register. More importantly, my ego—as delicate as a powdered donut—wouldn't let me hear my sister's needs whenever she'd rightly admonish me. Prideful and a bit embarrassed by my repeated thoughtlessness, I just made up a narrative that she is a diva, which she is, but for other reasons. *Just kidding!* Love ya, sis!

Lame dad jokes notwithstanding, if I am somehow conjuring this much resentment by forgetting my sister's dietary nonstarters, imagine what acrimony I'm whipping up with my partner when she reminds me time and again of the myriad details I somehow forget. Trash night (Tuesdays and Fridays), school holidays and half days, alternate-side parking days (Mondays and Tuesdays), names of teachers (blanking on so many), due dates, birthdays, date nights, deadlines, weddings, yet-to-be-purchased wedding gifts, yet-to-be-purchased airline tickets, christenings, get-togethers, shindigs, soirees, fines, fish fries, functions, funerals, hangouts, homecomings, showers, ballet class, modern dance class, recitals, soccer practice, family dinners (Sundays and Tuesdays, though last year it was Mondays), bath times, and finally, when to put the trash receptacles (recycling and all) back to their proper places (Wednesday and Saturday mornings).

The thing is, all that is *in her head*. Wife is my walking iCloud (not a good thing). I'm trying to remember more of the things I can't remember, but... I can't remember and would literally have to ask her—which definitely feels self-defeating.

Now, for better or worse, my sister is kinda stuck with me and my absent mind. She hasn't much choice in the matter as we are siblings, and my family doesn't really do estrangement (for better or worse). But my partner is a different story (I hope this is obvious). Partners don't have to stick around for our insensitive crap. And before you say, "Nobody's perfect" and run to the lovingly toxic embrace of self-pity and moral relativism, let me just say keeping *all* of the aforementioned daily details straight in my head at once evokes the story of Sisyphus, that poor bastard from Greek mythology who had to push a big-butt boulder up a hill every damn day for no good reason. And, yes, I just compared myself to Sisyphus over the idea of forgetting. Please forgive my martyr complex. I'm a recovering middle child. Anyone else?!

But the fact remains, *life be life-ing*! And my daily docket of to-do's always seem poised to overwhelm me like a cresting tsunami on the horizon. On any given Monday it feels like all my brain can do is brace for the unrelenting demands of modern life: to be in the moment but simultaneously seven steps ahead, to be productive but somehow *not* a workaholic with no time for their friends and family, and to keep it all together despite the headwinds of stress, world events, politics, climate change, processed foods, conspiracy theories, podcasts, KKKanye West, Trump, *Love Island*, Beyoncé, social media, the Kelce Bros, *and* Taylor Swift. It's a lot!

The scientific name for this near-daily balancing feat is *executive function* and your brain is doing it right now as you either read this very text or harken unto my lush-ass ASMR baritone. I mean, yes, you are reading this book, but you're likely thinking of other things too. I know I am. I cannot be that captivating! And if you are 100 percent committed to this moment, you should drop-kick Eckhart Tolle (metaphorically) and write your own book, 'cause I need those cheat codes, friend. But what is executive function exactly?

Good question. *Great* question.

If you think an executive function is a 1980s cocaine bash in a Wall Street conference room starring those lovable guys from Mergers and Acquisitions, change your answer. According to *Merriam-Webster's*, executive function is defined as "the group of complex mental processes and cognitive abilities (such as working memory, impulse inhibition, and reasoning) that control the skills (such as organizing tasks, remembering details, managing time, and solving problems) required for goal-directed behavior."

Essentially, executive function is our brain's natural capacity to meet goals via organization, memory, and discipline, which is great because I am terrible at literally all these things. To note, executive function is housed in your brain's frontal lobe and acts like an air traffic control tower, fielding incoming and outgoing information flows effectively (ha!) and efficiently (LOL!).

It's a fancy term for multitasking or the layering of one cognitive skill on top of another like a metacognitive, multitasking moussaka...until we invariably buckle under the mental load and twerk in our boxer briefs on the freeway amid oncoming traffic in the middle of rush hour on a random Thursday till the voices subside.

Now, here's a handy, everyday example of executive function in the wild. Let's say I'm at my little co-work space slogging through another chapter of this very book, and Wifey Slacks me to ask if I can grab fresh basil tonight on my way home. I scoff. Well in hand! And yet this task is Level Critical to the scheduled workings of Casa Carlos.

Is it a test? Unclear. (Read: yes.)

In any event, Wifey needs me to pick up the aforementioned greenage. That way, we can have pesto on the table by 6:30 p.m., kids in the bath/showered by 7:00 p.m., and asleep by 8:00 to 8:30 p.m. Wifey is scary serious about bedtime (not in a fun way) and reacts like a worked-up prison guard on El Chapo's cellblock if the kids dare violate this rigid timetable. So, I need to deliver on the basil.

Alas, Wifey has asked me to do this early in the workday (bad play), and despite my best intentions to remember to pick up said leafy roughage, I blank, fumble, and return to the homestead empty-handed. Palm to face, and feeling my wife's now nuclear glower, I hightail it to the store to grab what I've forgotten, but the damage has been done. Dinner plans get dented, and the evening timetable is thrown by just that much. No one dies, of course, but Wifey is less than happy—*I had one job!* What happened? Why did my basil run get lost in the shuffle? Is it because, deep down, I want to undermine and undo my relationship? Freud would say yes, but he was rumored to be a massive cokehead, so odds are self-destruction was likely his go-to answer.

Truth is, I struggle with multitasking, so much so that I earned myself the label of "absent-minded." Yikes! A dubious distinction, to be sure. Trust. You do not want to be that guy. It's a polite way of saying that you can't be relied on. Can't be trusted. Absent-minded.

Absent-mindedness is a euphemistic but no less insidious moniker because, in my opinion at least, it lowers one's standing and expectations within a relationship. Worse still, it can also chip away at your self-image and self-worth to the point where you find yourself spiraling and asking things like

"Maybe I am limited?" Maybe I *can't* be trusted? Maybe I am easily overwhelmed? Maybe I should just put on this lame sweater vest and khakis and await my partner's orders?

At the risk of histrionics, I would submit that by accepting the label of absent-minded, you essentially hazard gaslighting and infantilizing *yourself*, and thereby risking your own redundancy—somewhere you definitely do not want to be. That said, here's some good-*ish* news.

TURNS OUT WE ALL SUCK AT MULTITASKING

When it comes to cognitive skills, a preponderance of evidence suggests that there are some tasks in which women thrive relative to men and vice versa. For example, studies show women often outperform men in certain verbal abilities, such as remembering a list or other verbal content (preach), while men typically fare better at imagining what 3D figures would look like if they were rotated on their side. Take from this what you will, but in my relationship, I am the partner with fuzzy (zero) recall who needs the weekly grocery list tatted to his rib cage like I'm Guy Pearce in *Memento*. Meanwhile, my wife has the uncanny knack of getting lost amid the New York City grid system even though she's lived in the city her entire life! This is a sample dialogue of me trying to get her to understand the wonders of the New York grid:

Me: Babe, for the most part, even-numbered streets go east.
Wife: Gotcha, but which way is east, though?

Cue Jamaican air horn!!!

But what about when it comes to metacognitive skills, aka multitasking? The long-held stereotype maintains that women are far better at multitasking than men. Is that true?

I was struck by the findings of a 2019 Norwegian study where researchers tried a fresh approach to comparing multitasking skills among the genders (buckle the fuck up!). They immersed test subjects in a 3D VR environment consisting of a kitchen, a storage room, and a main room with tables and a projection screen. Participants were then directed to prep the room for a meeting. They had to place objects like chairs, pencils, and drinks in the right location while simultaneously dealing with distractions like a missing chair and a phone call (so relatable!). Subjects also had to remember actions that were to be carried out in the future, like giving an object to an avatar and putting coffee on the meeting table at a certain time, aka real-life shit!

Researchers intended to use this unique approach to clarify the findings and inconsistencies in past multitasking studies relative to sex. Some analyses, they claimed, found no sex differences, while others reported either male or female advantage. Further, the researchers theorized that the inconsistent results likely had to do with subjects being tested via artificial laboratory tasks that "do not match with the complex and challenging multitasking activities of everyday life." They added, "Another possible culprit is that different researchers define multitasking differently" (word!). In other words, what constitutes multitasking to a scientist probably doesn't constitute multitasking for a pit boss from Reno. Testing sixty-six females and eighty-two males between the ages of eighteen and sixty, researchers weighed whether or not subjects completed overall tasks accurately, the total time it took to complete said tasks, the total distance traveled in the virtual environment (were they efficient or not?), whether subjects blanked on any tasks, and finally how well subjects managed interruptions (phone calls, questionable air drops, etc.).

This is what they concluded:

> *We found no differences between men and women in terms of serial multitasking abilities.*... It is fair to conclude that the evidence for the stereotype that women are better multitaskers is, so far, fairly weak.[1] (emphasis added)

So, why do we say women are the better multitaskers?

I BLAME MR. MOM (SHOTS FIRED)

Hot take: Hollywood and Madison Avenue cannot make up their fucking minds as to whether men are handy or hapless around the house. The TV tells me men burn Oreos but also wants me to believe aggro chef to the stars and human blowtorch Gordon Ramsay can fix any restaurant, while zero-chill kitchen bully / strong candidate for therapy Bobby Flay threatens to crush anyone's grandma in a random bakeoff—name the place and name the crust, Nana!

If popular media is to be believed, menfolk cannot cook, but we are BBQ grill masters, too. . . . Huh? If some of the most renowned chefs in the world—José Andrés, Anthony Bourdain (RIP), David Chang, just to name a few—are men, and restaurant kitchens are unquestionably aggressively hostile male spaces (I'm looking at you Emmy-darling and comedy [?] *The Bear*), how in the natural hell is home cooking not something cis, straight men do? Make it make sense!

According to Hollywood, the mere notion of men being left to run the home solo is a risible punchline and a comedic premise premade to pack 'em into the local Cineplex. Tinseltown has a long and storied tradition of belching out zany romps about clueless dudes flung into the godless jaws of domesticity and thrashing about for a couple of hours or so for our nacho-cheese-drizzling, Raisinets-and-Goobers-munching amusement. After all, who doesn't love a classic "fish out of water" story with a side of narrow-minded messaging? If these grown-ass home-alone stories had a Mount Rushmore in the Black Hills of the Dakotas, it would include *Three Men and a Baby*, *Big Daddy*, *Daddy Daycare*, *Mrs. Doubtfire*, and *Three Men and a Little Lady* (because there was more story to tell apparently). Of course, the cornerstone of this frieze to man-flailing would be that early-eighties screwball classic *Mr. Mom*.

When I was a kid, my mom took me and my siblings to see *Mr. Mom* in the theater (because I'm ancient, but I do moisturize, so I look halfway decent). It was 1983, and in my family, we often went to the movies to escape the swelter and baking doldrums of suburban Dallas. I love my hometown, but outside of football and amazing musicians like Erykah Badu, Stevie Ray Vaughan, and the Dixie Chicks (or maybe it's just The Chicks now; I can't keep up), Dallas is pretty bereft of arts and culture (I can say that because I'm from there and did the damn work!), and that's why I was a little Roger Ebert by the time I was all of five (sweater vest and everything). To their credit, Dallas movie theaters were always top flight, with the latest in THX sound to blow out your inner ear canal as well as ergonomic seating and luscious AC. And when you compared that to what awaited you outside on a typical day in Texas—oppressive heat/smog, other Texans—the answer was always the movies.

On this particular trip, Mom's decision to watch *Mr. Mom* posed the question "What would happen if Dad stayed home to raise the kiddos?" Answer: Hi-*larity* and pure chaos!

I'll give you the rundown if you've never seen the movie: *Mr. Mom* was a star-making turn for Michael Keaton, who plays Jack Butler, a typical everyman aspirant to the American dream. One day, due to budget cuts (so eighties), Jack suddenly and unceremoniously gets axed from his high-flying auto-industry job and is reduced to running the house and caring for the kids as if his name was Betty Draper. And guess what, you guys?! He sucks at it! Meanwhile, Jack's wife enters the workforce and absolutely *th-rives*! She's a natural. But poor Jack is so utterly baffled and bemused by early-eighties household tech that he feels like a Neanderthal who took a wrong turn down a shaft in his Lascaux cave and wound up in Reagan's America. Keaton's character is so far removed from domesticity that he is perplexed and attacked by a washing machine and a vacuum cleaner named Jaws. A lot of his arc involves mastery of these two devices, which is weird because in the movie, he's literally an engineer who understands the inner workings of the internal combustion engine but is somehow stumped by a countertop popcorn maker. Go figure...

I'm not calling BS here, but *Encino Man* didn't seem to have half as tough a time negotiating life as Jack Butler, and Brendan Fraser's character had literally been thawed out of prehistoric ice. I'm guessing that the *Mr. Mom* Hollywood pitch session looked a little something like this:

Producer: So it's a movie about a guy who loses his job and has to stay home with the kids while his WIFE brings home the bacon...

Studio Executive: Whoa! Broads can work?! Since when?! That's so unbelievable it just might work! Is this science fiction?! Title?

Producer: MISTER...MOM!

Studio Executive: Done! Here's fifty dollars and a bus pass 'cause that's how much money it takes to make movies in 1983.

If Hollywood's offerings are to be believed, men cannot cook, cannot clean, and cannot strategize. And because we obviously can't do these things and are just overgrown children incapable of even the most basic household task—subtext: Men shouldn't be trusted or much less *expected* to do much of anything at home, right?—why would the late/great John Hughes, writer of *Mr. Mom*, lie to me?!

When it comes to domestic work, the learning curve can be steep indeed—that is, never have I ever put dishwashing soap meant for the sink in the dishwasher and created an at-home foam party. Also, never have I ever willfully put Tupperware in an oven and cranked that bad boy up to 450! In my defense, though, I put the Tupperware in the oven when I was asked to do so by my teacher. I was in the fourth grade and my brain had not yet fully developed (still lowkey waiting). The whole thing turned out to be a catastrophe, and in the end, two dozen pizza-bagel bites were ruined. But I put the question to you, dear reader: Should teachers be out there entrusting the baking of savory snack foods to fourth graders? That must violate some child labor laws, right? I digress.

As I was saying before I was so rudely interrupted by myself, I've always wondered why my mother took us to *Mr. Mom* when prior family trips to the movies involved watching films like *E.T.*, *The Fox and the Hound*, *The Sword in the Stone*, *The NeverEnding Story*, *Annie*, and *The Secret of NIMH*—kids movies comfortably nested in escape and whimsy. *Mr. Mom* was a departure. Something was up, 'cause Mom was definitely ordering off-menu. Like most things, I blame it on my siblings. My mom had just given birth to my baby sister in spring of that year. Before my sister came along, I remember my mother always being busy with her career as a college professor, but then there was a shift.

My sister made for three kids, and with my father's medical practice taking off and my mother making less money than Dad, Mom took the L and left her job to raise me and my sibs (you see where this is going). The years between when she left her job and when she eventually returned were kinda wild. Mom struggled to find something in Dallas to mollify her intense intellect. She was valedictorian of her high school class. She graduated college with honors and boasts an MFA in literature. She's intellectually curious, a rapacious reader, and a literary wonk. She also came up during the turbulence and upheaval of the 1960s, so it's safe to say that playing the part of a 1950s housewife must have been a massive blow to her identity. Her adjustment presented itself in a lot of different looks.

For one, Mom was constantly rearranging the furniture around the house. Then she randomly straightened her hair, which was a bit jolting for me, considering I was used to her hair being styled in something of a *half-fro*. And there was the time Mom went and got an ill-advised Jheri curl. I was shocked that she did this *after* Michael Jackson's Jheri curl famously caught on fire while he was shooting that fateful Pepsi commercial in 1984—that should have been cautionary tale enough! If it could happen to the King of Pop, why couldn't it happen to Hazel Lou Carlos? Maybe Mom thought pyrotechnics couldn't strike Jheri curls twice.

It's easy to see the appeal of a movie like *Mr. Mom* if you're a liberated woman who had to leave the workforce in the 1980s like my mother did. At least provisionally, Mom must have seen a bit of herself in Teri Garr's career ascendance, and I can just imagine her laughing at Keaton's domestic ineptitude. There, in the air-conditioned darkness of the AMC 5 at the Prestonwood Village mini mall, my dear mom could let the celluloid glow lap at her face as she escaped into a world of total role reversal, albeit for ninety-one minutes—credits included. A bygone era... or is it?

At first, I laughed at myself for thinking so deeply through such a clear pastiche of a movie... until I discovered *Mr. Mom* was rebooted as a short-lived TV show on Vudu in 2019. *2019.* I mean, it only lasted for eleven episodes on a streamer I've never heard of, but one thing was clear: Hollywood is still ready to risk it all on the hapless-dad trope. And if Hollywood is a barometer for shared cultural beliefs, it's safe to say we haven't come that far if this premise is still ripe for a reboot.

The myth that men are horrid multitaskers has definitely outlived its expiration date, and yet, like long-suffering Mets fans, we still believe. See science receipts:

In a 2015 study entitled "'Women Are Better Than Men': Public Beliefs on Gender Differences and Other Aspects in Multitasking," a majority of the 488 respondents (274 identifying as women, 212 identifying as men) were convinced that gender differences in multitasking existed, and at least 80 percent of subjects (of all genders) chalked up better multitasking abilities to women than to men.[2] *So, what are ya gonna do?* Conclusion: Despite the empirical evidence to the contrary, we are socialized to believe that women are the multitaskers as a result of cultural values. So, what's the harm in shared beliefs? The idea of money is a shared belief and that's worked out great for everyone, *right?!*

At the University of Melbourne, Dr. Leah Ruppanner explains her team's findings across multiple studies that "the birth of a child increases parents' reports of feeling rushed or pressed for time, but the effect is twice the size for mothers than it is for fathers. Second children double mothers' time pressure again and, as a consequence, lead to a deterioration in their mental health."[3]

I'm the second child, so you're welcome, Mommy! But do continue:

> Women are also more likely to drop out of paid work when children are born or family demands intensify.

> They carry a larger mental load tied to organising the needs of the family—who has clean socks, who needs to be picked up from school, whether there is enough Vegemite [gross] for lunch. All of this labour is at the expense of time planning for the next day's work, the next promotion, and so on.[4]
>
> Anything else?
>
> Women are also asked to multitask family demands at night. Children are more likely to interrupt their mother's than their father's sleep.[5] [**pulls at his own collar nervously**]

And just so we're clear this isn't only an Australian problem, in the 2020 *Global Gender Gap Report* published by the World Economic Forum, a group known for its whimsical content, researchers found the following fun outcomes for moms across Planet Earth:

> In no country in the world is the amount of time spent by men on unpaid work (mainly domestic and volunteer work) equal to that of women; and in many countries, women still spend multiple-folds as much time than men on these activities. Even in countries where this ratio is lowest (i.e. Norway or the United States) women spend almost twice as

> much time as men on unpaid domestic work... Even in advanced economies such as Japan the share of time that women spend is more than four times that of men.[6]

Not a pretty picture, and definitely a sobering argument for why we shouldn't leave all the responsibilities involved in running our home to our partners if we care about them. The toxic trope of the capable / do-it-all / go-it-alone mom will ferment like sourdough starter. And unless we pivot, that mess is just gonna keep bubbling over like a failed *Great British Bake Off* challenge!

Bottom line: Our partners need backup (in the name of mental health, y'all!). Now, at this point, some of you reading this are likely saying, "That sounds like a lot of work." But the reality is—in my experience, at least—surprisingly not all that much work is involved here. Mostly what's required is studying the playbook your partner is working from, and subbing in when needed. That's it. Just getting a handle on what your partner is going through can make a difference.

Personally, I don't have the bandwidth for radical change, but I do believe in the power of incremental change over time. And that is mainly because I am lazy. I wouldn't have been able to course correct myself if actual heavy lifting was even remotely involved. So let's start with some three-pound dumbbells.

SO, HOW DO I UP MY GAME? OR, HOW TO SLAY THE TOILET PAPER FAIRY

Before I go any further, let me just say congrats for whatever value adds you're already bringing to your relationship (maybe you're the fun one? Maybe you're great in the sack? Maybe you built her a she-shed with your strapping bis and lats?). I'm not here to chastise you for doing too little. I'm here with a few cheat codes to help you thrive and up your game. I am a firm believer in the notion that giving ourselves some credit for the good work we are already doing in our relationship is key, but there's always room to improve and refine.

That said, I want to address what tends to be a blind spot for me: the Toilet Paper Fairy. The lowliest of all fairies, this magical sprite deposits fresh rolls of two-ply every time we are running low. That way, I never have to call out for a fresh roll from the bathroom or suffer the indignity of either wiping myself with the scant remains on the cardboard spool (gulp!) or enduring the awkward pants-about-ankles bunny hop to the pantry for more TP. Ever done that only to learn that you are out of TP completely, only to settle for a paper towel, only to find out you're outta that, too?! *Me neither!*

The TP Fairy is a mythological figure concocted to deride a partner for being oblivious to the efforts of the other. "How did the new roll of TP magically appear?" Answer: The TP Fairy. And if it wasn't clear enough at this point, the TP Fairy is your long-suffering partner.

The TP Fairy is just one in a constellation of domestic celestia. Don't forget the OJ Fairy and the Coffee Fairy and their good friend, Milk Fairy, and their annoying vegan cousin, Nut Milk Fairy. If any of these not-so-cute fairies have taken up residence in your home, take note because, more than likely, underneath this sarcastic joke is a malarial swamp of resentment and passive aggression and, depending on emotional pH levels, antipathy, so let's kill this cute little fairy tout de suite.

Now, I quoted Sherlock Holmes at the beginning of this chapter for a reason. Above all else, Holmes's edge rests in his keen sense of observation (and his preternatural tolerance for liquid cocaine—bazinga!). What you're going to do is emulate this supersleuth (not the liquid cocaine part, though!). How? Well, consider your nose for a moment. Chill. It will be worth it. And note: This is not another cocaine reference! Though I could understand how you'd think it is because I literally just referenced cocaine and now I'm talking noses. However, you can talk noses without talking cocaine. It can be done. Read on.

Unless your name is Cyrano, you likely won't see your nose unless you close one eye.* Go ahead. Try it. It's kinda fun. I'll wait.... And it's not so much that you can't see your nose as much as your brain conveniently ignores it. As far as our brains are concerned, our noses are just kinda in the way, so our brains literally act like our respective beaks ain't even there.

---

* Cyrano de Bergerac—main character from the famous play of the same name, who has a massive sniffer.

Our brains are trained to literally not see certain objects, objects that are sometimes (you did this!) as plain as the nose on your face. So if it stands to reason that the brain can be conditioned to pretend like your nose isn't there, what else has it been conditioned to ignore?

Here are a few examples to get you started: blinking, your own breathing, the feeling of your clothes on your body, and background noise. There's actually a scientific term for this. It's called *unconscious selective attention* and it's basically our brain's spam filter. So if your brain is blocking out things like blinking, breathing, or even the weight of sunglasses on your nose and ears—I'd hazard that's not all we're ignoring with our unconscious selective attention, or "USA" for short. No possible joke there! How about that brimming bathroom waste basket? How about whatever's living under your bed? Maybe the underwear on the floor or the rug that's been askew for days?

But it's not all bad news. We can also switch off our brain's autopilot function, too. Our breathing can switch from involuntary to voluntary if we so wish. If you don't already know that, our schools have failed you. Year 2025 jokes aside, to switch from automatic breathing to manual just takes a bit of mindfulness. It's that same mindfulness you use to listen to the conversation behind you at a party to see if anyone is out there talking shit. We are all very capable of doing this because we do it every day. We can all switch off our spam filters to get a fuller picture of our surroundings.

When I switched off my spam filter, I suddenly realized that in my house, at least, milk and OJ just don't magically appear in the fridge, and TP doesn't just show up near the shitter. Someone (Wife) puts them there, of course, which means it's time to go on a stakeout.

You're going to clue in on when all these things happen.

Don't ask.

Just observe and report on the following:

CHOREPLAY INVENTORY

1. Check on the TP levels in the bathroom(s). Is another roll needed or do you need more TP for the house altogether?
2. Check on how much there is of the following in your fridge and add them to the grocery list if any are running low:
   - Milk
   - Butter
   - Eggs
   - Juice
3. Learn which day of the week is trash day. Is it different from recycling day?

4. Learn which day is groceries day.
5. Learn which day of the week your partner waters the plants, provided you have them.
6. Learn when your partner regularly walks your pet (if you have one) and how many times per day your pet is fed. Also find out if your pet is up on its shots.

Bonus: Here are some ways to give your person an executive function breather. Pick one:

*Make up the bed in the morning**

Empty the dishwasher

Empty the trash / recycling / composting (or whatever else we're doing now)

Pick up meds

Load the laundry

Do laundry (Google it if you don't know how)

Fold the laundry (Google it if you don't know how)

Put laundry away (Bask in your wash-and-fold glory)

---

* Even if you're first out of bed, do this and it will be one less thing for your partner to think about.

JUST THE TIPS, PLEASE

- Executive function = our brain's ability to manage tasks and responsibilities.
- It's BS that women are better multitaskers than men. TV, movies, and social media often portray men as inept at household tasks, which just creates a vicious cycle where men don't have to help out around the house because the culture tells us we're hapless.
- Turns out, a lot of the mess you don't see may be as plain as the nose on your face. Don't stay in spam mode.

Chapter 5

ASK MOM

SOME DAYS IT FEELS AS THOUGH ALL DOMESTIC ISSUES AND concerns channel to and flow through my partner—like she's been sucked into this bizarro reality, of sorts, that can only be described as a remix of a classic scene from Martin Scorsese's *Goodfellas*:

> "Problem at school? Talk to Mommy."
>
> "Kids need to go to the dentist? Fuck you. Talk to Mommy."
>
> "Something went bump in the night? Fuck you. Talk to Mommy."

Wifey is the front line and the go-to. In the previous chapter, we discussed how *science proves* that kids choose to wake up Mom at night over Dad. Mom is the go-to. She is often the default or what author Eve Rodsky would call the "she-fault" parent.[1] Meanwhile, I am in the rear, chilling in the court of last resort.

My kids really don't come to me for much of anything other than reaching the things on shelves my Lilliputian wife can't. By comparison, I am definitely the dust-covered backbencher, the second-stringer there for auxiliary support. My wife, on the other hand, is playing the whole game of life without a breather. For instance, in the middle of the school day, if one of the kids suddenly falls ill or busts their knee, who ya gonna call? *Not me!* If a playdate or a slumber party is in the works, who ya gonna trust with the logistics of it all? *Same answer!* If one of the kids is too sick to go to school, who's gonna stay home with them even though I'm a sometimes-employed comedian who writes jokes at a co-work space? *Bazinga!*

And like any first-string all-pro QB worth their salt, my wife knows the whole family playbook cover to cover (she wrote it). As the dependable one, she's also become my family's version of Google Cloud; a brain trust of one, she keeps a firm hold on the factoids and figures, dates, and deadlines crucial to the Carlos Clan. She knows our kids' doctors (Tribeca Pediatrics). She knows their dentist (Name Redacted. Obviously). She, of course, knows the names of all my kids' teachers and coaches, too. I am ashamed to say that in writing this chapter I really have to dredge deep into the nether regions of my bean to come up with the names of my kids' teachers. I see you, Ms. Mila, Mr. Dennis, and Mr. Yehuda! Before you judge me, though, please know that I'm not as bad as another dad I know who literally did not know the name of his son's school! *How you not gonna know the name of your child's school?*

In my wife's capacity as IRL Google Cloud, my kids rain down questions on her like she is a beleaguered White House press secretary. She fields two-part questions, tricky three-parters, gotchas, and untold buckets of follow-ups. The only things my kids are missing are press-pass laminates.

The frenzy of queries becomes particularly pitched whenever Wifey is busy on the computer or locked in on a call. This is the moment when her attention is most fragmented, and the kids know it. If Mommy is tied up on a Zoom call, my kids see that as the optimal time to ask if they can watch some damn *Bluey* or chow down on diabetes-inducing num-nums. Overwhelmed and overrun, my wife often caves to my kids' incessant lobbying so that our pushy, persistent crumb-snatchers will give her some modicum of peace. Of course, the kids could have fully asked me the same question (that part) as I am usually standing right there, but they prefer to go to HQ for the answers. Why ask Dad, right? He might say no. Or worse, he might confer with Mom, grow a spine, and *then* say no.

THE BLACK WATCH

It seems like my wife can never get a moment's rest, though—not even after bedtime. Since my kids were born, my wife has also handled what I like to call "the Black Watch"—those freaky-ass predawn hours when our kids' little bodies betray them. This is the hour that last night's feta cheese revolts and blasts out all over my kids' newly cleaned *Paw Patrol* sheets.

And after our sick offspring raise a hue and cry for mama, Wife gamely dives into the breach. Like a member of an elite Formula One pit crew, Wifey dutifully springs from bed and triages the sitch: Befouled cartoon sheets are stripped, baking soda is secured and generously applied, the bedroom is cleaned and Febrezed like a *CSI* crime scene, offspring is soothed and put back to sleep. And more often than not (you guessed it), yours truly is in the deepest of REM sleep, dreaming about swimming with cyclops neon dolphins while smoking fat bowls alongside national treasure J. B. Smoove, or some such nonsense. Here's the worst part, though. My side of the bed is closest to the door. Logically, the kids should come to me first. Despite that fact, the children still take the long way around in the darkness, stand over my wife, and stare at her until she wakes up in a panic. Poor Mom.

Don't get me wrong, I am called on in the night here and there. I'll never forget the night my young son did his best Linda Blair impression in that classic projectile-vomit scene from *The Exorcist.* My wife woke me. It was too much for even her. Somehow, her iron-clad, snub-nosed, seen-it-all Brooklyn constitution had buckled under the crushing stench of curdled mac and cheese, Tater Tots, orange juice, and hot bile. I was up. It looked like my son's stomach had been pumped and then sprayed all over his bed, rug, and seventy-plus stuffed animals (he's a completionist). But before I could take it all in, I slipped in the lukewarm vomit and did a full Charlie Chaplin pratfall back-first into the putrid yuck, which caused me to involuntarily retch and nearly add to the gross myself. Too much? Just painting a picture!

Now, I'd love to say that I didn't hold that night up as proof-positive that I am a massive help around the house and all that stands between my family and certain chaos, but I'd be lying.

I have a habit of outsizing my relationship contributions. Anyone else? And yet, if my name isn't the first name my kids call in the middle of the night, it's pretty clear I'm the spare, not the default. Exorcisms notwithstanding, if I am roused in the middle of the night, it's primarily to check on unsettling noises, allay my wife's justified anxieties over the status of the myriad locks and windows in our little New York City home, or dispatch any quadruped (raccoon), hexapod (bug), arachnid (spider), barking dog, or dog and/or dreaded deer tick. Given all that, it comes as no surprise, I'm sure when I tell you, dear reader, that my wife has an up-and-down relationship with sleep. Nighttime can be fraught AF when the kiddos keep popping up like so many Whac-A-Moles and your partner is conked out like he huffed a whole can of ether.

But how did we get here?

ALL THAT GLITTERS

When Wifey and I first cohabitated, I took night watch. She was the one who slept soundly. Any bumping and/or thumping that was not of the amorous variety was in my purview. Then kids came into the picture, and shit *changed*. Wifey breastfed both kiddos; as a result, she got up as many as two or three times in the middle of the night. Subsequently, we switched places, and it's been that way ever since.

At first blush, this seems like a pretty ideal arrangement for *moi*, right? If my kids have questions or concerns, they just go to the she-fault, while I am free to kick it. My kids don't trouble me with their little-kid concerns. They trust Mommy with them. My kids have my wife's telephone number memorized. Until recently, I could not say the same about my info. I had to drill those digits into their cute little skulls. Fortunately for them, though, they were blessed with my wife's brains and picked up my number quickly, but I can't say it didn't give me pause that they didn't know how to reach me.

This dynamic isn't a rarity among comedians, though, and it's something I've struggled to overcome. As a comic, you have license to stay out later than most other adults. At times it can feel like the best of both worlds. You have a wonderful partner and a comfortable home life, but you also get to be in these streets (albeit provisionally!). After a show, you can go out for drinks with friends! You can explore new cities, meet new people, and enjoy the ecstasy and agony of fourth-meal fare that you will undoubtedly hate yourself for later, not to mention the glamour and glitz surrounding the entertainment world. There are premieres, red carpets, panels, festivals, award shows, and, well, *celebs*! It can all be so dizzying. It's so frenetic, in fact, that in the pitch of all that excitement, I hardly noticed that show by show, late night by late night, and tour by tour, resentments were slowly bubbling within my relationship, which is reasonable to expect if one partner is out of the house more often than the other.

The homebound partner wants the other to thrive, sure, but they also want *you*.

That part.

In the rush of my epically myopic paper chase, I couldn't afford to be home. Something had to give.

Stand-up comedy is among my favorite art forms, but I don't think people know just how toxic the business can be to one's personal life. I've known comedians so committed to their craft that it's cost them friendships, relationships, and marriages. Just recently, I did a gig with another comedian who told me that they had given their child over to their ex to raise. Years prior, this same comedian and I had swapped stories about the joys and pain of parenting, and now, with fame beckoning, they'd literally given up their kid to keep themselves that much more unattached for whenever their big break finally materialized. This comic is not alone. I know another very successful comedian who did the same thing.

They are quite happy, it seems, with the comforts and validation surrounding commercial success. This is their choice, of course. And I am not the type of person who believes that these comedians will one day regret their decision to estrange themselves from their families who may or may not put them in a home when they're old (OK, kinda I do).

It's just not for me, and yet, it is something that is dangled in front of entertainers constantly. Comedy is a tight-knit community. Comedy clubs are just that—clubs. The social aspect of these establishments and the needs of succeeding at the job often demand that you build stronger bonds with fellow comedians and club owners than with your own family. And whether you're a comedian or an ichthyologist or an assistant to the assistant rodeo clown, we've likely all been here, in one way or another.

To advance in our careers, we're presented with what we feel is an either/or proposition. Either we commit fully to our vocation, at the expense of our relationships, or hazard missing out on the big time (whatever that means to you). That gnawing FOMO can be so strong it can invert judgment altogether. As F. Scott Fitzgerald wrote of his titular character, the dreamer-turned-bootlegger Jay Gatsby, there are times when our dreams are "so close that [we] could hardly fail to grasp [them]," and all other cares and commitments fade to the background.[2] I couldn't reasonably be expected to worry myself with whether or not we needed more two-ply when I was writing jokes for Comedy Central or hammering out bits for the White House Correspondents' Association Dinner. *Hell nah!* I was gonna leave that to the she-fault. I could not be bothered.

This was my MO for years, until it literally could not be anymore.

GAWD WERKS IN MYSTERIOUS WAYS

If anything, experience has taught me that much. Period. Roll credits! Stand by for the reboot and limited series spinoff.

After the short-lived sitcom I was on got canceled (not cool!), and the double-decker writers' and actors' strikes wiped out any remaining showbiz opportunities, I was thoroughly unemployed and not in a fun way. Meanwhile, things at home were fraught AF. The entire production of this single season of a defunct TV show had put my relationship on the brink. I had been so taken with the remote possibility of TV stardom that I had abandoned virtually *any* domestic responsibility whatsoever. I was gonna be a big star, right? So what if I had blatantly foisted any and all family duties and obligations onto my partner with zero concern or consideration for their feelings or mental load? Fuck it! Fame would be my absolution, right?... Until it truly was not and I was just another out-of-work comedic actor locked in a downward spiral of self-pity, blame, and bitterness with a partner who deserved much better. I'll skip to the end and tell you that Wife and I did not break up, and the sitcom did not break us (ultimately my snoring will probably do that).

Looking back at it now, unemployment was an incredible gift in the worst possible packaging, like a gold bar stuffed into a stinky turd. Prolonged and profound unemployment did what therapists and commercial success could not. It made me get comfortable with my own discomfort. With my usual relationship escape hatches sealed off, I had to turn and confront the responsibilities I had so coyly evaded these many years. Suffice it to say, my marriage would not have survived a second season of that show. I see that now. It pains me to say it, but I was lucky that the show was canceled. Otherwise, I'm pretty sure I would have been just one more entertainer who had thrown the family over for their fortune. It's like Rosie Perez told young Woody Harrelson in *White Men Can't Jump*: "Sometimes when you win, you lose, and sometimes when you lose, you win."[3] And I'm not trying to spin my failures into successes (OK, fine, I am a little LOL). But—point-blank—had it not been for Bob Iger and the calamitous events of 2023, Wifey and I would not have made it. Still, the fact that the woman in a partnership so often becomes the default manager of domestic life isn't simply a function of a man's absence. The architecture of our culture—quietly, persistently—steers us there. And if we're going to find a way through it, we have to first be willing to look at it. So: Stay with me.

DEFAULT MODE AIN'T ALL YOUR FAULT

Society, man...

Quick story. Cards on the idiomatic table here. The more I write this book, the more I find myself upping my choreplay. On any given day, I'm up early packing the kiddos' lunches, making their breakfast, and getting them up, dressed, and ready to go. I'm doing my best to take my own advice here! As I leaned into the play of chore (yes, I am desperately and perhaps successfully trying to make this a thing!), I began to look around and ask what more I could take on. I started getting curious about when my kids were due for the next visit to the dentist, for instance. This was a total first, of course. I have taken the kids to the dentist at my wife's behest, but never have I ever cared enough to commit brain power to minding my kids' dental hygiene beyond barking at them to brush their teeth at night before going to bed.

So, feeling myself ever so slightly, I hazarded a call to my kids' dentist to determine when they were due for a checkup. We were heading out of town at the end of the month, and I just wanted to make sure my daughter's never-fun visit to the dentist did not get lost in the shuffle. Don't worry. I'm so oblivious that I had to search for the place on Google Maps because I couldn't remember their dentist's name. I knew it was in our neighborhood, and I remembered the cross streets. With these limited data points, I could pinpoint my kid's dentist, who they had only been going to for about five years.

I will say this till I am blue in the face: There is no better time in history to be a trifling-ass dad like myself. Times past, I would have had to use what's known as a phone book, or worse—ask my wife! Thanks, Silicon Valley! Back to this very riveting story. Anyway, I got through to the dentist's office, and as it turned out, my daughter was scheduled for a checkup before we left town, which was news to me. Then I asked about my son. He didn't have an appointment but was also due, so I scheduled a time for him to come in, too. As I am patting myself for making this catch, the receptionist tells me the following:

Receptionist: You know, the mother knows all this already.
Me: Oh, OK.
Receptionist: Yeah, the mother knows.
Me: OK, well, I'm the dad and I want to know, too.
Receptionist: Oh, so you guys are divorced?
Me: (*recovering from this*) No, I just didn't know what was going on. Only moms call about their kids' teeth?
Receptionist: And divorced dads...

There's a lot to unpack here, but for one, it felt like this particular South Brooklyn receptionist was anything but *receptive.* I couldn't help but feel I wasn't even welcome to inquire about my own kids. And I don't know what it is about medical professionals and kids, but in my experience, they seem none too pleased when the dad is the one taking the child in for care.

For instance, my daughter was visiting the doctor recently about the possibility of having a procedure to fix her outie belly button (*Now the world knows!*). Now, I had an outie as a kid, and in my case anyway, I just did a lot of crunches starting in the seventh grade, and the damn thing went in like a shy turtle. Anyway, I take my daughter to the doctor to check on this incredibly elective procedure and what does the nurse say? "Where's Mom?" Yeah, where's Mom indeed, lady? For all she knows, Mom could have run off with the Juggalos!

Look, I get it. A lot of dads don't show up, but *some* do. We don't want a ticker-tape parade for it (we totally do), but we also don't want to be called out with weird questions like "Where's Mom?" And giving this nurse the benefit of the doubt since she was a little older, I had a passing thought at the time she asked me this that she was maybe having a senior moment, like, in effect, she was asking, "Where's *my* mom?" or worse "Where's *our* mom?"

I may not know where we keep the scissors, and I must be reminded to feed my own dog, but, Nurse, I got this! The she-fault/default parent is a cultural phenomenon that takes a concerted effort to create. All genders work together to perpetuate this one. We are all of us socialized to think that matters of the home and family are the domain of women, not men, and then we *all* reinforce this norm (women included!). That's the dirty little secret no one wants to talk about.

For instance, my son has asthma, which gets super active during spring and fall. As such, he's a fixture of the school nurse's office. He's basically Norm from *Cheers* but in the school nurse's office. Everyone knows his name! But whenever he has an attack, I hear about it secondhand, though I'm pretty sure that my contact info is right there alongside Wifey's on my son's medical forms.

Or how about whenever I pick up my kids from a school event or after-school activity, there's always a certain... tension? Here's how my offspring greet me when I arrive: "Where's Mom?" My kids will ask me, not "Hey, Dad!" just, "Where the fuck is Mom?! Did she fall down a sinkhole?? Where is our mother, old man?! Answer us!" Nothing makes you feel as validated as your kids asking you the whereabouts of your partner when you see their precious faces. You feel almost too wanted (sarcasm). Worse still, sometimes the call is coming from inside the house!

Sometimes it be your partner jealously guarding their title as she-fault like Smaug guarding their gilded treasure (where are my nerds at?). And even if your person chafes at the label, sharing any piece of that mantle may well be a nonstarter. It's difficult, after all, to give up a long-held self-image or belief, especially if it centers us as the keystone. Also, if your person is the relationship linchpin, and then suddenly you want to chip in to share the load, it could present a difficult existential question for them: "Who am I if I'm not doing everything?" Your person might even hate being the responsible one all the time, but alas, it's the devil they know.

My wife was doing it all by herself for so long that I can tell she's still not completely sure she can trust me with more details and more responsibility. Imagine wanting your partner to do more around the house, but not being sure you trust them to, so you continue to go it alone despite the resentment and dysfunction of it all. Sometimes, in the name of results, we accept a veritable Rube Goldberg machine of dysfunction because, despite its myriad inefficiencies, flaws, and headaches, the system does deliver, albeit with a side of toxic waste. So how can you even begin to right this ship before it plows dead into rocks?

And maybe you can't ever fully disabuse a defaulter of the thought that they need to be the cornerstone 24–7 (still trying), but I can recommend the following to perhaps encourage a pivot.

WATERSHED

As mentioned, a floundering comedy career has been a godsend to my relationship. The phone doesn't ring and ping like it once did. Offers have stopped coming, and comedy has decided that, for whatever reason, what I'm selling is a hell no. But as a comedian, I have an advanced degree in such rejection. It's like an old friend at this point. So, rather than let it get the better of me (literally my favorite thing), I decided that just for variety's sake, I would reframe this difficult moment into a golden opportunity. Now that I was definitely home and going nowhere, I came around to Wife going out with her girlfriends multiple times per month, or if her girlfriends weren't available, she would take herself out and enjoy her own company. Though it is an ongoing adjustment, at least at the time of writing, it is working.

Now, before you say *must be nice*—yes, I know. It is. I'm acutely aware that not everyone has the bizarre luxury of a career fizzling out just in time to discover that domestic partnership runs smoother when one of you is suddenly always home. But the main win here wasn't the choreplay—it was the strange, slow bloom of realizing I had nowhere to be but here. Though I was scared that Wife would stay out until the dead of night like me, it turns out she is something of a lightweight who rarely ever stays out past eleven. And on the days when she just needs to have an afternoon cocktail at a prime people-watching perch, she's almost always back by dinner. Whatever fears I had of our dynamic swapping were due in no small part to my own projections and insecurities that she would abandon me as I had abandoned her. My wife is her own person, of course. Her idea of a good time isn't always the same as mine. She isn't a night owl... namely, because growing up in Brooklyn in the 1990s, she'd already been one.

Yes, my wife was one of those latchkey kids portrayed in the cult classic *Kids*. No one really cared when she came or left or how long she stayed out as long as she kept her grades up. She was smashing blunts on Brooklyn stoops by the time she was in the seventh grade. My wife is a much more interesting person than I will ever be, but she's also a very committed parent and partner who just needs a Negroni and an unvarnished view of the skyline every now and again. Simple pleasures, folks.

Of course, my partner going out and taking time for herself comes with unanticipated outcomes, namely, my kids don't love it. When my daughter comes home and doesn't see her mother about, the first question she asks is "Where's Mom?" Not "Hi, Dad." Sometimes I don't tell her until she gives me a proper greeting, but the message is clear: Mom is the GOAT, and the house just ain't the same without her in it.

They're not wrong, but they also need to let Mom have some Mom time, too.

THE DAD CHAIN

So, in the spirit of choreplay, I did the unthinkable, and I recommend you do the same.

First, rather than depending on my partner to regularly disseminate information to me about school matters and the like, I started a *dad* text chain of my own.

And this is where I lost them...

But before you hurl the book and/or iPad into the corner, hear me out. 'Cause I get it now. And the squeeze of interacting with some random dad(s) is certainly worth the juice.

After some aggressive recruitment of the dads in my circle, I established a whole father-to-father text chain...of two. Is it sad AF? What part of the two-person dad chat wasn't deeply depressing upon reading? I'm still not sure that the other dad understands that it's a strictly school-related text chain, but I will take what I can! Not only is our chat one full of dumb memes and photos of our kids (is there any other kind?), but also, via this informational organ, we've kept each other up to speed and in the loop about school events. That bake sale? *I got that!* Talent show? *We out here!* The end-of-year party? On it like a bonnet, *and* with the heads-up, I was able to bake homemade Southern teacakes with lemon zest (which zero kids ate, but that's beside the point!). My wing dad is tremendously awkward and—*OK*—a little offbeat(?), but (1) he is willing, and (2) this is not about making friends!

Since we started, we've done a pretty good job of reminding one another of upcoming field trips. We've spared one another from being blindsided by random school holidays, clued each other in to volunteering opportunities, and so much more! Sure, the setup may not be ideal, but like a Rube Goldberg machine, it gets the job done. Because in the end we saved each other from being *that guy*—clueless and redundant. Believe me when I say that it's better on this side of choreplay! Knowledge is power. I don't have to default to my person as much as I once did, which comes as a welcome relief to both of us.

And once you've tasted the sweet, smug satisfaction of actually knowing what time pickup is (2:45 p.m. every day), it's hard not to want more—especially when the world reacts like you just parted the Red Sea with a diaper bag. Have you seen the lopsided response a guy gets for pushing a stroller down the street or carrying his toddler on his shoulders? People smile at him like he's Jonas Salk! I'll never forget walking down Wall Street with my children one beautiful summer morning. The sight of me holding my kids' hands as we went down the street was enough to make a woman smile at me like my name was Michael B. Jordan! I was like, "That's all it takes?! Holding my kids' hands?" Look, obviously, it's unfair that men get more credit for showing up and parenting, but as I said before, I am not here to upend or reinvent anything. I'm just saying that metaphorically there is a lot of money that men are leaving on the table. If you could get treated like a goddamn hero for holding hands with your kids as you cross the street, why wouldn't you? As I said from the start, the bar is so low. Until the world actually ups the stakes on men, enjoy the Canyon of Heroes ticker-tape parade you get for doing the "thirteen pieces of flair" bare minimum.

JUST THE TIPS, PLEASE

- Don't make Wifey the she-fault parent. You don't have to go 50-50, but also do something. Between 0 and 50-50, that's you! That's where you want to live.
- Suggest nights out for Wifey to see her friends or even hang out solo. She'll likely come home D.T.Fornicate…
- Initiate a dad text chain. Godspeed.
- Men are praised for what women do on the regular, so enjoy that perk.

Chapter 6

THE ONE WHERE YOU FACE THAT YOU'RE NOT A KID ANYMORE

When I was a child, I spoke as a child, I understood as a child, I thought as a child; but when I became a man, I put away childish things.

—1 Corinthians 13:11 (NKJV)

LEMME JUST SAY... *BARS!* THANKS FOR THESE NUGGETS, PAUL/ Saul of Tarsus (or whatever your IG handle is today). Tip of the cap, friend. I heard this ditty a lot in church as a kid, and it's tattooed to my long-term memory, especially when Paul/Saul waxes, "But when I became a man, I put away childish things."

We can all relate to that, right? To one extent or another, all of us have put away our childish *thangs*, no? Remove your head from the gutter... I mean, I no longer play with action figures or RC cars or train sets, Nerf or water guns or video games. I don't climb trees (in this economy??) or roll down grassy hills, slide down slides (or up them!) or swing on swings... *unless* my kids do it. *Then* it's OK, right?

Yes, I am that guy. Between me and my partner, the aforementioned recovering she-fault from the previous chapter, I am the dreaded Fun One (FO), and I relish that title (red flag).

Fun One gets down on the floor and plays with you. He builds intricate paper airplanes with you. On demand, FO pretends to be a monster or a dissatisfied Karen (one and the same, actually). They attend tea parties and allow "experiments" of dubious scientific merit. They fully engage in water balloon melees, snowball fights, and wet sandball battles or explore the enchanted woods or craggy shorelines replete with slews of tide pools bursting with all matter of fauna. Fun One binges *Bluey* with you. They camp with you. They make flapjacks over an open campfire, too. They let you sit on their lap when they're driving short distances in a slow-ass golf cart down a country road. They're literally a kid with a checking account and a job. Not bad, right?

Growing up, there was no greater joy than playtime. There was no greater rush than that kind of world-building. To me, the best thing about child's play is the renovating, retrofitting, and repurposing of the physical world into a world of pure imagination (shouts to Willy Wonka). I love it when chairs become time machines, beds become flying taxis, and brooms become Stratocaster guitars. So, when my kids ask me to play, it makes my heart skip a beat. They are including me and our bond is getting that much stronger. They trust me to bring the fun, whimsy, and imagination. I love that.

We have such wild times, the kind that adults only seem to achieve with mind-altering substances. As an adult, how often do you get to sing crazy improvised songs until you're blue in the face if you're not on something? When do you get to assume another persona as an alien from Planet Zorbak all while being stone-cold sober? Sometimes, dear reader, my kids and I will even go into a crazed fugue state of nonsensical chanting and braying. The squealing and laughing and the glee give us all such a rush of endorphins and dopamine that likes on social media could never!

I've got it pretty good. My son considers me his playmate (flex). Part of me *loves* that. The other parts of me are fucking exhausted! I'm well into my forties, and some days, it feels like my body is held together with so much Big League Chew, butcher's twine, and painter's tape. Whenever we do a day at the beach, I pack a book. I don't know why 'cause that shit never gets read! 'Cause the minute we hit the sand, here comes my son. "Dad, will you build a sandcastle with me?"... "Dad, will you bury me in the sand?"... "Dad, will you play tag with me?"... "Dad, I'm about to wade into a tide of man o' war. You better stop me!"... Got-damn, Malcolm! I just got here! Whenever my darling son makes these asks, my wife will say the same thing in a singsong intonation that claws at the inner reaches of my brain: "You don't have to say yes," she'll mutter—*like I have a damn choice!* With a sigh, I don my metaphorical red clown nose and hop to.

Such is the price of being Fun One, though! To misquote Bruce Wayne, "F-One has no limits."

But if I am Fun One, that relegates my partner to Fun Sponge. Fun Sponge does not camp. She doesn't build sandcastles (humbug!). And she certainly doesn't climb on the jungle gym despite a fairly decent health insurance plan with reasonable co-pays and low deductibles. Get this: If we're on the beach, she gets out a book and . . . reads! Who does that?!

Fun Sponge is what is known in some cultures as a "grown-up." She has put away her childish things and replaced them with to-do lists and calendars (yikes!). Fun Sponge is the enforcer. I can count on my hands the number of times I've said "It's time to go home" over the course of our relationship. As Fun One, I could go all night. No booger sugar required. Meanwhile, Fun Sponge checks the clock and is ever mindful of how we're getting home as well as what tomorrow's schedule holds. Fun Sponge craters the whole devil-may-care vibe with her endless concerns and to-do's. They're literal monsters!

Fun Sponge tells our children that they can't be on screens all day, that they've watched enough *Simpsons* reruns (which is impossible, as they predict every major world event), that they most certainly cannot have ice cream because they had it *last night* (so??), that they either clean their room or *fuck around and find out!* Who wants to do that?! Not me! Sometimes, Wifey seems to be taking her Fun Sponge cues from that nineties show *Scared Straight*, wherein hardened criminals frighten the bejesus out of at-risk youth to keep them from following the same path. To her, the game is not a game! Now, only recently did it dawn on me that maybe, just maybe, my wife wasn't a Fun Sponge because she resents other people's happiness (she does that because she's a native New Yorker, ayoooooooo!!) but rather because I have left her that role to fill. As Fun One, I'm too busy doing donuts in the parking lot of life to enforce much of anything. Meanwhile, Wife is quite literally doing the work of two parents, trying to keep our household from spiraling into indulgent mayhem.

HOW DID WE GET HERE, THOUGH? A MANCHILD ORIGIN STORY

Our respective attitudes toward structure and routine reflect how we were raised. Wife grew up amid much more disorder than me. She is one of four kids reared by freewheeling, hippie parents in the burnt-out, graffiti-spattered New York of the 1970s, '80s, and '90s. In some ways, her parents saw the notions of strict order, organized religion, and whatever else *da man* was selling as destructive to the spirit of the individual and free thought. Wife did not share in her parents' attitude. She was a little kid in a big, noisy mess. Order was her escape and her means of rebellion.

I, on the other hand, if you've been following along, grew up amid the bland mayo-and-graham-cracker suburbs of Dallas, Texas, where lawlessness and disorder were things that we heard about on the evening news or that entertained us at the Cineplex. By comparison, my upbringing was Pollyanna. Church was often twice on Sunday, Tuesday, and sometimes even Wednesday—*Stop being so thirsty, Jesus!* Dinner was on the table promptly at six, and on Saturday mornings after cartoons we did our dreaded chores, when my brother and I would strip our beds, clean our shared room from top to bottom, and bring our laundry downstairs for washing. *Thundercats* aside, our time was never really our own.

Every moment seemed claimed in the name of responsibilities and to-do's. There were dishes to wash and clothes to press and iron. Either the lawn needed cutting or weeding or both. We even had to set out extra time on Saturday night to prep for church on Sunday morning. That's when we broke out the freakin' shine box, buffed our penny loafers to high polish, and read over our Sunday school lesson. We were that family! Like the Flanders family…but Black! And with a childhood crammed with starched collars, curfews, gospel music, and so many rules, fun—not control—would be my rebellion.

Also, in the spirit of unpacking, I think part of me has always feared being as serious as my father once was. My dad has mellowed into one of the coolest, most easygoing people I know, but he was a supremely serious figure when I was a kid.

You did not want to be on his bad side. He could be brusque and quick to anger. He put in long hours and didn't really engage in small talk. His own upbringing was fraught AF. Dad is a self-made guy whose family had money and then lost it when he was ten.

As I mentioned earlier, my dad took on the Sisyphean task of putting himself through medical school while working assembly lines in Detroit auto plants, slinging hash at after-hours diners, teaching calculus at a community college in Mississippi for a year, and even tending bar on the side, all while staying the hell out of the Vietnam War (no easy feat!). The guy has literally fought and scraped and struggled for every yard in a life that has reasonably hardened him. Yet despite that hard exterior, there were times when he would let his guard down and lose himself in the joy of his kids. He loved to wrestle me and my siblings. These impromptu matches always evolved into all-out tickle fights for our lives! Dad, a former high school wrestler, snapped us into viselike grips and tickled us until we nearly raptured. I loved Dad when he was like this, and somewhere along the line, I think I decided I wanted to be that fun *all the time*!

So there you have it. My partner and I have arrived at two very different attitudes toward structure and routine as a result of our two wildly different childhood experiences. Soooooo, which style will win out?! Well, that question reveals a lot more than the answer.

CLOWN PRINCE RISES

Of course, in a side-by-side comparison, Wife sometimes does make it all too easy to be a Costco-sized funzilla. For instance, she's said under no uncertain terms in our kids' respective-ass faces that she will never step foot in Disney World. Raised without a TV in the house, some capitalist institutions will forever remain nonstarters to her. To each their own. I have a different relationship with The Mouse, though, and suffice it to say that I would have zero trouble taking the kids to the Magic Kingdom. Keeping it a buck, it would be me returning to the Magic Kingdom and my kids pretty much tagging along!

Potential forays to Disney properties aside, whenever my kids ask to go somewhere special and Wife demurs, I can feel a devilish grin crackle across my face and my fingertips touch like I'm C. Montgomery Burns. My moment arrives. I have zero chill, y'all. I make a big show of picking up the flag and gamely offering to do what Wife won't. 'Cause where Mama's myriad strengths end, mine begin.

All too often, I have relished in the moment my kids' cherubic smiles fall just a little when their long-suffering mother rejects their appeals to take a random ferry ride to Governors Island or a trip to the kids' museum (where we would, no doubt, visit exhibits on prehistoric kids) or even a trip to the much loved but in no way convenient Lego Store. I let them stew in the mom-created rejection, and then from out of nowhere, I swoop in and *save the day* 'cause some heroes don't wear capes, y'all! This is when the clown prince aka Fun One aka F-One aka *Formula Fun* swings into action! And what *doesn't* Fun One do, y'all?! Can you tell I'm eager to share?

What we not *gonna do? Chores!*

Velociraptor bones at the Museum of Natural History for the umpteenth time, anyone?! *Yezzir!* IMAX planetarium after? (N'yes, please!) *And* then *Invisible Worlds* immersive holographic show in the new, new wing? (Yahtzee!) A kiki with the got-damn butterflies, and a visit to *The Squid and the Whale* for all the indie film fans out there (who's your guy?!). Next we hit up another random "museum," like the Museum of Mother-Clucking Ice Cream! *'Cause Mom would never!*

But we ain't done.

Dad's out here serving up memories 'cause we are going to hit up Central Park next like it's our got-dang job! Bethesda Fountain, where you at?! Paddle boats—what's really good?! And when that's done, you know what's next! We are crashing Serendipity 3 for an onslaught of burgers and, hmm... maybe more ice cream deliciousness followed by a ski lift ride across the East River to Roosevelt Island for that priceless view of the Manhattan skyline 'cause Formula Fun knows the best views of this city come from the outer boroughs. And that ski lift is the same one from the original *Spider-Man*—the Sam Raimi one! Fun One has got you!

Oof... I'm outta breath but enjoy the view, and just answer one question for me: *Who's more fun—Mom orrrrr me?*

I've asked my kids this question before, and seriously, it's not a good sign. It reveals that all this fun isn't really about my kids.

Twist!

It's about me.

FUN PO-LICE ARRIVES

As the saying goes, "If you roll thunder, you're gonna crash like lightning." Good times have to end at some point, right? So, what about the inevitable, cursed comedown? What about when we have to put the toys away or we gotta turn off the TV or teeth need brushing 'cause they are code yellow or clothes need to be put on 'cause the ding-dang carpool is coming?! Somehow, during those more serious and sober moments, Fun One is out like skinny jeans. Enter Fun Sponge aka *da po-lice*, who brings all the army-of-one / no-knock-warrant thunder to bear (likely 'cause Fun One ain't backing them up!). There have been times when Wifey has had to come down with a metaphorical shibboleth, dashing any and all the ice cream dreams with sprinkles on top and squelching the collective dopamine rush in one fell swoop. Like the Kraken called forth from the deep, Wife appears and straight fucks up the whole vibe with a deliberate quickness. I'm pretty sure

Wifey doesn't enjoy executing these raids, but then again, I don't leave her much choice in the matter. Somebody has to. In short, Fun One with all their unhinged chaos actually creates the job of Fun Sponge. That's right. Your guy is a job creator.

Does she want to be the bad cop? Nerp.

In fact, Wifey often tells me she loves hearing me and the kids at play. It brings her joy, too. But parenting is a job, and someone (not I!) has to do it.

When it's time to be a disciplinarian, I can't stand to see the pain etched on my kids' lil faces—the tears and the snot bubbles and shit. Why? Because I feel like it's happening to me (it isn't, thank you, therapist). So, what do I do?

Rather than let go of the pain of the past, I act out. I drown it in sundaes and blown bedtimes and pillow fights and pillow forts and baseball games and (slumber) *parties and bullshit and parties and bullshit and parties and bullshit!* But let me make three quick points here:

1. My partner deserves better.
2. Being the fun one 24–7 is tiring AF.
3. Everyone knows what you're doing, especially *dem kids*!

My precocious tweenage daughter has an uncanny knack for cutting me open with a pithy yet no less insightful remark.

She is the roastmaster general of the family. It's her superpower and a terrifying harbinger of what's to come (pray for your guy!). When she told me recently, "Dad, you're the fun one because you don't say no," it cut me to the quick. The kid could see what I was doing. She might as well have just said, "This man is a fraud! This man is a full-on fink and a phony!" BTW, what is a fink anyway?! Please let me know in the comments.

Look, if this sounds anything like you, you must know this dynamic is untenable. And I must admit, keeping my *id* in check is an ongoing struggle. It is a discipline, but it can be done. I mean, as the late / somewhat-canceled Dr. Seuss would say, "It's fun to have fun, but you have to know how."[1]

Fun, for its own sake, is one thing. But my children will be adults far longer than they are children, and I've already wasted enough time not being fully present in their childhood. This is my last best shot at chopping it up with them while they're still little and the sun is shining on their darling faces.

Fun as a weapon in the psyops PR war for the hearts and minds of our kids is another thing entirely. Who knew the act of having fun could be so fraught like that?!

So, what do you do? How do you finally put away your childish things?

I say, little by little by lot.

When my daughter told me that I was only the fun one because of my inability to say no, I took it to heart. Not only did I feel found out, as though my Sideshow Bob mask had been torn from my dumbass face, but it was also something of a relief because I was not going to stop on my own. After she said that, I tried something novel.

One day my kids asked Wife if they could go to Urban Air, an area indoor trampoline park where I have been known to bounce on the tramps with the kiddos like a goddamn maniac instead of tending to the children's coats and hats, et cetera, and small-talking with the rest of the sad-looking parents about school shit, allergies, and summer plans for the umpteenth time. With a heavy sigh, Wife declined, and then, for the first time in a very long time, so did I.

As my kids' shoulders reflexively slumped, I felt a chill creep up my spine. My heart raced. It felt like the moment would not end. My inner child was *not* having it. I'd like to tell you that Wifey surprised me and saved the day with a board game or an impromptu kabuki performance, but that didn't happen. The moment. Just. Passed. (Ugh.)

I sat there in the disappointment of it all, but guess what: I *survived.*

And though I didn't say no outright to my kids, I said no to Fun One, and that's a start.

At that moment, I actually backed my partner (for once). WE said no. I did not undermine her. If you ever find yourself in a similar spot, I suggest you do the same.

CHOREPLAY AS A RESULT OF SEARCH HISTORY—A FIRST

I cite credible sources in my writing when I can. But if you notice, aside from the Good Book and Dr. Seuss, I didn't do that in this chapter. Why?

When I googled "Fun Partner," the top results were all about co-parenting...and divorce. Not a single tip on board games or date nights—just custody schedules and emotional resilience. I tried variations: "Fun Dad," "Fun Parent," "Fun Spouse." Same deal. Every road led straight to Divorceville. It felt less like a fun Google search and more like the universe handing me a manila folder labeled "Irreconcilable Differences." Note to self: Play too goddamn much and even choreplay can't help!

In short, at least according to the internets, the appearance of Fun One means acting like a toxic divorced partner *while* married. What an unavoidable sign. If I want to stay married (I do), I need to stop acting like I'm divorced. Stop being that dad who scoops the kids up on the weekend in his two-wheel drive late-model sports car and takes the offspring out for kid-appropriate benders. Lesson learned.

Nowadays, I tap the over-the-top energy I reserved for playtime with the children for playtime with Wifey. Turns out, she loves to do kid stuff like trips to Coney Island, bowling, roller-skating, ax-tossing, you name it. And she *really* likes to do these things with me—just one on one. Who knew? My partner loves me because I *am* fun. She's told me as much. In ways, I'd been withholding that fun side from her out of petty resentment and scorn. Because if you know what upsets your person, then by God, you know what makes them happy, too. It's really as simple as that.

If you're weaponizing fun against your partner, you know that including them will make them happy. So dispense with the shit and do that.

If fixing my marriage has taught me anything, it's that rather than engaging in a proxy war with Wife over winning my children's hearts and minds, I needed to essentially take Fun One and violently drown him in a bathtub. After my inflection point, I realized I had to accept that I was fun and I could be fun as a partner to my wife.

Here are a few small-bore practices to initiate in your relationship starting today in the event you, too, play too goddamn much:

- **Watch the clock:** Be the one who says it's time to go home. Stop leaving the role of timekeeper to your partner. This is such easy money.
- **Present a unified front:** When your partner says no to kids, friends, or other family members, side with them (if only in the moment). Don't undermine.

- **Be the Reaper:** If you see a toy on the floor and it shouldn't be there, do something revolutionary—pick it up, or tell the cute little cherub to help.
- **Label your shit:** Whether it's a phone charger or your favorite book, put your name on it and/or in it. My wife labels all of her stuff and makes me respect her sense of ownership. I've always told myself I'm not allowed to have the same. Bottom line: All that changed when I got a label maker!
- **Plan a fun date for you and your person:** Your person likely still wants to have fun, as they continue to have a pulse.
- **Bonus:** When you're doing your necessaries, remember the TP and forget the phone. When I don't take my phone to the bathroom, I'm in and out like a NASCAR pit crew! As a Texan, let me say bathrooms are where you escape from tornadoes, not life.*

---

* And if you think I'm being an alarmist about this, allow me to direct you to a pretty revelatory 2018 survey of 1,000 British males conducted by British bathroom outfitter Pebble Grey that revealed that on average men spend seven hours annually in the bathroom to specifically seek peace and quiet. Primary reasons for spending this long in the loo included escaping nagging partners and avoiding chores (gulp). And 14 percent of respondents even reported stashing books and food in the bathroom, too. I'm afraid to ask, but as a gender, we can do better than stashing Snickers bars in the toilet tank, right?

JUST THE TIPS, PLEASE

- Being the fun one creates a vacuum wherein your partner becomes the responsible one. Congrats on casting your person as Fun Sponge.
- If you know what pisses off your partner, you likely know the blueprint for what brings them joy, too. You've got the schematics. Just reverse engineer your way to happy.
- If you're already acting like you're divorced, don't act all surprised when you get served. You've basically been method acting the breakup this whole time.

LEVEL TWO

LOOK AT YOU ON LEVEL TWO! IT FEELS LIKE WE WERE KIDS WHEN we started this journey. Now look at us! Back in Level One, we talked about finding time in our busy-ass lives to course correct. We talked about the function of executive function and rounded things out with putting away our childish things. So you know before you go, this next level is all about taking care of you. Think of this portion as the mind-body playbook.

In this next portion of *Choreplay*, we'll discuss self-care, exercise, diet, sleep hygiene (because apparently that's a thing?), and how forty-eight rolls of TP may well prove to be your love language. We're going to explore what role putting your health and well-being first plays in the health and well-being of your relationship. Bottom line: If you want your relationship to thrive, you've gotta stop treating yourself like the office printer—ignored, overworked, and one jam away from total meltdown. Let's get into it.

Chapter 7

F**K SELF-CARE

I HAVE A WELL OF COMPASSION FOR SO MANY PEOPLE IN MY life, namely, my wife, my children, my siblings, my parents, my relatives, my friends, my loved ones, my coworkers, my acquaintances, total strangers, certain celebs, various Pixar characters, defenseless animals, and even folks on my shit list. Way, way down on that list and past all those examples, you might find me, too, depending on the day. To put it bluntly, I have more compassion for my enemies and frenemies than I have for myself. If you recall from all the way back in Chapter 2—that one about putting your mask on first—*that ain't right.*

As a recovering people pleaser, I tend to put others' needs way ahead of my own. What that often looks like is me dropping whatever I'm doing to fully smoke-jump into someone else's crisis. I help friends with their messes and struggles at the expense of my own time. Devoid of any paywall, I often help friends prep for auditions, workshop jokes, or proofread whole-ass manuscripts. At the risk of pandering, I've even paid off a buddy's college loan. Of course, when I cosigned on that loan, I never thought that I'd be the one paying it off, but dreams do come true, y'all!

I don't blame them, though. If I even directed a morsel of my generosity toward myself, I would be a fucking menace! For some reason, though (lack of self-esteem), I never ask for the same in return.

It's a serious issue, so let's get serious to solve it. Then it's back to Dad Joke Island!

"You shall love your neighbor as yourself" (Mark 12:31).[1]

In a sad turn of events, my neighbor passed away recently. It was sudden. I absolutely loved this guy. Anytime he comes up, I can't help it. I get very emotional.

He was a beautiful soul—a 9/11 hero who welcomed my family with open arms when we moved to the quiet Mayberry-like community of Bay Ridge, Brooklyn. Handy, kind, and generous, he was a fixture not only on the block but also in our home. He expressed his love and warmth by fixing whatever needed a little TLC. In our house, that was pretty much everything. My wife and I have never owned a house before; ours was nearly one hundred years old when we bought it. The old heap has more issues and dysfunction than *Vanderpump Rules*, y'all!

But from plumbing to roofing to gardening to wiring, Marcel was in the chat. We leaned on his advice and in his sweet, avuncular way he would nudge us down the path to stewardship. On top of all this, Marcel not only administered first aid to my wife when she had a serious reaction to a beauty product but also saved our little house from burning down when the other adult in the house, who is definitely Not Me, tried to broil bacon (not advised!).

All in all, this loving father and grandfather had zero haters.

Then one day, he was gone in a flash—something I am still trying to work through. Soon after, my neighbors and I decided the least we could do given all that Marcel meant to our little Brooklyn block was to name the street after him in dedication to his legacy of love and kindness to his neighbors. But this was not going to be an easy task. As they say, "One does not simply march into Mordor."[2]

Just to secure one small commemorative plaque on a tiny street no longer than a quarter mile, my neighbors and I would have to contend with the uncaring, impenetrable, Byzantine workings of New York City bureaucracy.

After living in New York for over twenty years, I can tell you that it ain't hyperbole to say that New York is a godless, dispassionate dream killer unbothered by time, tide, or sentimentality. These days the city seems to concern itself with things like the scourge (?) of unlicensed weed spots or its unending and futile war against the indomitable rat population—they will rule us all someday! It's just a matter of time!

Like a Wall Street deli before the opening bell, the line for city services is out the door and down the block. Despite the long odds, my neighbors and I banded together and pressed on. To start, this was not easy work. Survival in NYC is a twenty-four-hour job as it is, so concerning yourself with a cause—no matter how personal—comes with sacrifice in a city this demanding. You can't so much as get a stop sign installed without negotiating a morass of alphabet-soup city agencies and a layer cake of red tape, so why even bother, right? Who needs the headache?

It took a hardy trio, including my assistant and my neighbor Mary-Alison, to knock on doors, gather letters of support, and document stories of Marcel's life and legacy at the FDNY. Marcel was more than a 9/11 hero, which is a strange thing to say, I am aware, but he was built different. Years ago, while battling an apartment fire in Greenwich Village, Marcel convinced his crew to forgo the standard practice of running roughshod in a burning home in the name of expediency and to instead use as much care as possible because he recognized that the apartment belonged to a young family that Marcel knew from around the neighborhood. The family owned a local stationery store and their young daughter loved to inspect the firetrucks and visit with the crew every time she passed the station. How could we not honor someone who carved out that much room in his heart for others?

We lobbied the City of New York and its soul-crushing and inhospitable bureaucracy for nearly five long and dispiriting years before we finally achieved our goal. There were plenty of times when I felt like giving up and the way forward was not clear. It was not easy, of course, but we loved our neighbor that much. As I write this, I am pleased to say that Marcel's commemorative plaque finally went up on a beautiful day in spring of last year. It only took nearly half a decade, you guys!

As a Christian, I was taught to love my neighbor. But that "love thyself" part of the passage always felt like more of an afterthought. And as I researched for this book, I looked for passages in the Bible that spoke to self-love. After thorough Google searching, I am here to report there really aren't any ('cause I couldn't find any). Also, major sidenote: I am not a theologian. Turns out, I am a comedian who makes somewhat elevated fart jokes. Do not get it twisted.

But I see now that I took from the aforementioned verse in the book of Mark to love your neighbor, only. I leaned into that. I never learned to do that latter part, aka love myself. So I've decided to risk full-on heresy and just flip old Mark 12:31—*remix!*

Heretofore Imma just say, "Love *thyself* as you would love thy neighbor."

Now, y'all, if my chronically pleasing ass showed up for myself the way I showed up for my loved ones, I said it already and I'll say it again: I would be a fucking threat to national security. I shudder to think of how insufferably self-assured and self-possessed I would be. I would be a TED Talk come alive! So, what am I getting at?

The Buddha famously said, "You yourself, as much as anybody in the universe, deserve your love and affection," which is a sentiment I gotta get tatted just above my left butt cheek.[3] For the sake of this book (and my marriage), I decided I would actually give intentional self-love a go. But like a lot of disciplines, self-love has gone hella sideways as of late, and the self-care movement has definitely nose-dived into absurdity so deep that it's hard to see it as anything more than high-priced overindulgence. If the Buddha could see what was being done in his name, the great one would likely never stop throwing up. Have you seen what's become of self-care? Has anyone done a wellness check on wellness? She got her tats removed and went completely corporate.

The overwhelming array of treatments, gadgets, apps, and toys aimed point-blank at us all through our phones touting "best life" status is too much to process. It's a geyser with no kill switch—and that's not what we're aiming for. Thanks in no small part to a cocktail of Silicon Valley and late-stage capitalism, self-care has transmuted and transmogrified, presenting in its newest permutations as 24K gold face masks, bird poop or caviar facials (or both!—whatever blows your hair back), and candles that smell like Gwyneth Paltrow's junk. What a smorgasbord of useless ephemera! But don't worry.

If you're turned off by the material, and you see wellness products as little more than inflated trinkets and tchotchkes, new-jack corporate opportunists are gunning to capture your money in the realm of the spiritual, too. For you know we are truly through the looking glass when former underwear model, rapper, and action star Marky Mark is out here peddling an app to help you, well, pray.

Really? Pray? Now, I gotta *pay* to pray? What does the Funky Bunch think of all this?

Let it be known that putting a wall of any kind between you and your creator—specifically in Christianity—was, in no small part, the impetus behind the Protestant Reformation. In the most "Drunk History" version of events, activist and critic Martin Luther didn't think you should have to go through an impenetrable hierarchy like a messed-up game of Telephone. Besides, *er'one* knows that to talk to Yahweh (Oprah), you just get down on your frigging knees and close your peepers. What's so hard about that?! No person or paywall should be coming between me and my maker, least of all Mr. Wahlburgers!

Whether we love spa days or prayer baths, these days we live in a world where we also sweat what others think of *our* purportedly intimate acts of self-care rather than savoring these moments for ourselves. At this point, I'm not sure we even know how to have moments to ourselves without an audience. As Cicero said over two thousand years ago, "Nothing is so ridiculous as to exhibit one's own prosperity in a manner that excites the envy of others."[4] But what did he know, right?

Let me just say here that I'm not trying to disparage anyone making coin in the self-care game. I see you, fitness trainers.

The personal development market alone, which includes self-care elements such as coaching and personal training, was valued at around $45.92 billion in 2023 and is expected to grow to $67.02 billion by 2030. Get your coins! The industry will survive this blistering attack from a somewhat-known comedian who made a few shows on MTV in the 2010s. But I would be remiss if—since we need to address rampant people pleasing—I didn't say that the baseline *idea* of self-care has become little more than escapist indulgence or bad-faith money grabs under the guise of spiritual fulfillment.

The real work of truly loving on yourself is pretty grimy and doesn't look good on Instagram.

SELF-CARE'S UGLY SISTER

There is another self-love, though, much less sexy, a bit off-brand and down-market. Nothing is fun or appealing here. In fact, I'd call it the jury duty of personal maintenance. It's all the vital stuff you *really* don't want to do, and likely would risk death to avoid.

It's going in for a yearly physical without urging.

It's going to the dentist to hear the truth.

It's going to therapy even if you think you're fine (is anyone these days?).

It's brushing your teeth twice daily, cutting your hair without your partner's urging, and eating your goddamn vegetables like Hulk Hogan told you to.

It's sitting in waiting rooms and filling out forms and pissing into cups and drawing blood and praying your insurance covers the visit (debatable).

Like jury duty, this brand of self-care is often avoided at all costs, but unlike jury duty, you can't get out of it by claiming you're a galloping racist. Of course, cis, straight men know how to care for themselves in a bevy of ways, but none too good.

We know how to kick up our feet on the sectional and admonish young, apex athletes for not performing poetry in motion while we simultaneously scarf down boneless wings like goddamn *pashas*. We know how to drink all the beer, smoke all the weed, and watch all the porn. As a demo, we have that in a headlock. But what about caring for our carcasses? *Ruh-roh*...

I wish I took care of my health the same way I take care of my car. (A theme is a theme, even if you forget it for a second!)

I like my dad-wagon. It likes me back. I take my car in for service regularly. As I write this, my ride has a little over 67,500 miles on it, and I haven't missed a single scheduled maintenance milestone. Do I deserve a parade for this? No, you're SUPPOSED to bring your car in for maintenance! Not into the dealership, of course, 'cause they will hose you. I live in New York, so *I gottaguy!* But it's not my whole car that breaks down. It's going to be a flat that takes me out because I keep the engine purring like a Big Five jungle cat in the Kalahari. Are you picking up on my self-satisfaction?

Of course, part of the reward that comes with taking good care of your car is the sublime schadenfreude of watching other drivers pull up to the auto shop in their coughing, sputtering buckets of doo-doo, gears keening and wailing like some dying beast of burden praying for a kill shot to the brainstem to end its suffering. I can't help but sneer a little. I would *never* let things get this dire (with my car).

I wish I could say the same about my bod.

Sweet Baby Jesus in swaddling clothes! When it comes to going to the doctor, I am basically that 1991 Geo Prizm staggering into the greasy mechanic's service bay on hope and vapors. But again, as a cis, straight dude, I am not alone.

Masculinity can be super confining. It stops me from asking for help or directions. Don't believe me? Just look at Moses. Dude famously wandered in the desert for forty years without once asking for directions. That's a case study in toxic masculinity right there! And if your masculinity can keep you lost AF in the desert for forty years, there's no doubt it can keep you from finding your way to the doctor.

I'm sure it comes as a surprise to no one that, statistically speaking, American men tend to visit the doctor less frequently than American women. I know what you're thinking: "Girl ones are better than the boy ones.... Blah, blah, blah. But can they write their names in the snow with their pee?! Riddle me that!" Look, don't take this personally. It's literally just math. Now, receipts are as follows:

Forty percent of men don't go to the doctor unless they're experiencing a serious issue. Men are also twice as likely as women to wait more than two years between doctor visits. Why? Maybe some of us want to come back with a few anecdotes for our primary care provider. *Hey, developing a good story takes time, OK?!*

Personally, everything about visiting the doctor makes my butt pucker: the disrobing, the probing, the fuss, the insurance! I'm sure I speak for a lot of men when I say going to the doctor triggers my fear of being vulnerable and exposed as anything but invincible, even though I have all the Adamantium coursing through me. The amount of vulnerability inherent in a checkup messes with men's fragile notions of masculinity and machismo. Perhaps doctors could invest more in cedar paneling and/or ESPN in the waiting room to cater to our brittle egos. Who knows? I mean, that's the horror that awaits IF you even get an appointment in the first place. Not to mention, the last checkup most of us men had was when our mom handled the scheduling.

TAKE YOUR VITAMINS, NOT YOUR CHANCES

Like most kids in the eighties, I formed my feelings about medical care while watching *Predator* (I'm different). Early on in the film, elite, mercenary, and all-around 1980s badass Senator Jesse "The Body" (maybe "The Mind," I can't keep up) Ventura is injured and bleeding apace. Jesse "The Body" or perhaps "The Mind" Ventura's mercenary coworker notes that Jesse is leaking blood, at which point Jesse "The Body" possibly "The Mind" says, "Ain't got time to bleed."[5]

The message was clear to me. Real men let it bleed. True men of the manliest order just let that shit coagulate / potentially let sepsis set in. Looking back, it's funny to see to what extent this brief, random movie scene informed my attitude toward pain. To be sure, *Predator* sits atop the Mount Rushmore of 1980s and 1990s machismo flicks like *Rambo* and *Lethal Weapon*, which likely influenced plenty of other boys like myself. We grew up thinking we didn't have time to bleed! So is it any wonder why men break down faster than the latest iPhone? (*There goes my brand partnership.*)

Simply put, men must finally and respectfully disagree with Jesse "The Body" / "The Mind" in his assertion that there isn't time to bleed when, actually, there is, and that is precisely what we need to give ourselves. Also, in all fairness, those weren't even Jesse's words. They belonged to legendary screenwriter Shane Black, who the Predator tore up like a coleslaw about fifteen minutes into the movie. Spoilers! *Got time to bleed now, Shane?!*

All this to say, we need to take the time to take care of ourselves and value our health, unless of course you're being hunted for sport by a godless killing machine like the Predator. Then, ya know... Do you.

On top of that, I have a bad association with doctors. No, my family was never home-invaded by a marauding band of blood-lusting gastroenterologists on whom I vowed vengeance. Let's start that rumor, though!

I resisted going to the doctor because I nearly died on the operating table when I was thirteen. In the seventh grade, I was diagnosed with scoliosis, which if you don't know is an irregular curvature of the spine. Then, because of growth spurts, my curve started to resemble something akin to San Francisco's famed Lombard Street, so my parents elected for surgery, which was... involved. The surgeon had to open my whole-ass torso, fuse my spine, and insert something called a Harrington rod, which is kinda like braces but for your vertebrae, so no presh! The operation was a complete success... except for the part where my lung collapsed like bootleg crypto and I nearly beefed it, and this kind old lady who was also undergoing the same surgery, with whom I'd exchanged pre-surgery pleasantries, actually did bleed out on the operating table. *Yeahhhhh.*

As I was told, my doctor had double-booked that day but decided to perform both surgeries at the same damn time like his name was Gucci Mane. Regrettably, dude was no multitasker. But aside from having to negotiate the subsequent trauma/survivor's guilt *and* having to learn to walk all over again, it was a pretty mellow summer, you guys!

That messed-up experience left me scarred both physically and emotionally, and just as this childhood trauma was starting to fade from my memory, Fate decided it was not having it.

One random day while I was on a business trip, some twenty years after my fateful surgery, the brace that was inserted into my spine just slid out of place and sorta freely roamed around my bod, floating down my guts past a few major organs until finally coming to rest in my hip, where it remains today. Yes, while it was happening I was seeing triple and I thought my appendix had burst, and yet I *still* did not want to go to the doctor because I remained very much messed up over my nearly botched spinal surgery two decades earlier. I literally opted to die in my hotel room instead. The last thing I remember thinking before everything went black was, "Well, at least I had the love of a good woman..."

Then I woke the next morning in my hotel room and the pain was gone. Was this the afterlife?!

'Fraid not.

I did not know it at the time, but the Harrington rod had come to rest in my iliac crest, which is fancy talk for hip socket. When I relayed this episode to Wife, she told me to go to the doctor like a normal person. I caved and did as I was told.

Fearful of finding out that I had mere moments to live and no living will or trust or whatever you're supposed to have (I feel like I'm always getting it wrong!), I explained to the very kind doctor what had happened. He listened patiently and took X-rays. His reaction to those X-rays did not renew my faith in professional medicine, though. He looked at my chart and drew a very puzzled face. "Huh. Now what is that?" he asked, pointing to a shadow on the film. After I picked up my jaw (after all, I came to him for answers, not questions!), I rightly told him that it could be my Harrington rod, which by the looks of things had entered its free-range era. He asked me if I was in pain. I told him that I wasn't anymore. I asked him if he could remove it. He said he could and all that it would require is that he open me up and potentially dislocate my femur, *but on a temporary basis*. . . . And it was at that point that I looked out into the middle distance and stopped listening. I told the doctor I would follow up with him (ha!).

It's been eleven years since this happened, and he's still waiting for that follow-up. I feel fine. The rod does not hurt, but as I stared down the barrel of my mid-forties, I told myself I had to face certain realities. The men in my family have a long and sordid history of beefing it relatively early. We seldom reach our eighties like the hardy, long-limbed Glamazon women on my mother's side. If I wanted to reach that boss level of life, I had to revisit my lasting childhood trauma (fun!).

Trauma aside (yeah, let's just go ahead and put that trauma over there for a sec), I would say that among the less obvious reasons why I don't visit the doctor on a regular basis is because my mother no longer makes my appointments and my wife doesn't either. Yeah, that part.

So, maybe you don't have some giant trauma story around medical care, but maybe you're one of the majority of men who needs their mom or (shouts to Sigmund Freud) wife to make appointments for them.

I mean, without women to make medical appointments for me, I went a cool twenty-five years between trips to the dentist. Not too shabby! When I finally pulled up to the dentist (who I feared most, incidentally), I got the awful news that after only brushing once a day, never flossing, and barely using mouthwash, I had the beginning of a single cavity. Holy shit! That was all?! Beforehand, I was almost certain I wasn't walking out of there with my maxilla.

The same was true for my other bodily checkups, too. My eyes were as blind as ever and my bod was in decent enough shape. Although my doctor did warn me that at my age, my warranty had in fact expired and there was no AppleCare to be had. So, I was fine. What a relief! Holy hell! It was nice just to know that. And, I'm sure we can all agree, it's best to learn if the opposite is true. As irksome as wellness visits and checkups can be, "guesstimating" your health is like playing with fire. Look, I'm all for surprises! Just not the ones that come with whopping medical bills and hospital bracelets.

I am forever thinking that something is slowly metastasizing in my bones (could be), but for now, I'm good! Which left only one more bit of business for an aged fart like myself—baby's first colonoscopy, which is scheduled for later this year. Yes, I cannot wait for the doctor to probe the depths of my b-hole in the name of good health. Colonoscopies should not be as embarrassing as all that, but let's face it, they are, and what doesn't help is when the doctor tells you that you need to have a friend take you home after the procedure. What a great way to bring me and one lucky friend a lot closer.

Look, I think a Swedish massage or a foot rub are all well and good, and you should indulge in them here and there, but these fun little treatments will do even less to address what we do our damnedest to avoid.

The body needs capital *C* care. Much like my preowned Honda CRV, we require scheduled maintenance. Now, I should share here that I don't only get my car serviced because it gives me a feeling of self-satisfaction, though that is literally 99 percent why. But it's also because I am not the only one using that car, and as such, I feel like the others deserve the best level of maintenance I can possibly provide.

My partner deserves the best. That's always been my MO, but you know what: So do I. *I* deserve a car that runs like a top, just as I deserve a body that runs like a top, too. Good health isn't for others. It's for me, too. And the tedium involved in securing optimal health for myself is worth the pain. I am worth the vulnerability and the bureaucratic headaches that constitute the American healthcare system—and you are too.

QUICK FIX

We live in an age when tech can truly save even my trifling ass (and also totally spy on you, six of one and half dozen of the other, y'all!). Our phones tell us how many steps we've taken in a given day. Our overpriced watches tell us our blood oxygen level. And (provided you're lucky enough to have health insurance) there are apps to keep you up-to-date on health appointments. And perhaps the craziest part about men *not* going to the doctor, ever? Even as a lot of us have insurance, with low premiums, low deductibles, and low co-pays?! But I digress...

A few years ago, I heard my friend (a woman) joking about this app one night during her stand-up set. I thought it had such a funny/catchy name—"Zocdoc." Fast-forward a few years, and I am in the midst of trying to reorganize my life. I go to the app, and though it's by no means perfect and definitely has a few bugs to work out, Zocdoc keeps me on point. It reminds me that I might have gone in for my physical this year but I also need to see the optometrist, too.

If you're not already familiar with this miraculous tool of the modern era, Zocdoc offers a list of local, wonderfully in-network doctors to choose from. And once you've gone to your appointment, the app offers users the option to book another appointment at the same time next year. And that's the best part. It essentially does what Mother used to do, what Wife will not do, and what I fail to do. And maybe that's the lesson here.

I'm not sponsored by Zocdoc. I'm not asking you to really do anything all that seismic, either. Literally, all I'm telling you is the work is already done. Just download a free app and do what the flight attendant instructs—put on your oxygen mask before helping someone else put on theirs.

I would also say it's important not to mistake the kind of self-love I am talking about for adolescent self-absorption. I'm talking about prioritizing your health and well-being because you're worth it (welcome to my TED Talk), not engaging in overly indulgent stuff like lying on the couch all day (despite your partner's glares) or staying up all night playing video games (nothing good ever happens after midnight anyway) or online gambling or watching porn or __________ [fill in the blank].

These types of behaviors are regressive, adolescent dopamine bursts, and with the exception of maybe online gambling, I've tried them all (who hasn't?). What I am getting at is a deeper love of self, a tough love that allows us to follow our better angels. I guess I'm asking you, dear reader, to cheat, really. Cheat on your indulgent ways with dry, uninspiring checkups.

I'm not asking you to make checkups the marquee aspect of your life (snooze), but I am asking you, for the sake of your relationship and in the name of all that is holy choreplay, to make it a legitimate feature. And it's nice to know we slackers actually have to change only by degrees now rather than doing a total one-eighty, twelve-step program where you gotta call all the people you dicked over in the before times.

I mean, how hard is it to download an app?

So, here's the takeaway. It's very difficult to do something monumental for ourselves. Generally speaking, we do not have the patience, discipline, inclination, or persistence required. Writing this book has been the most amount of healthy attention and time I've given myself since I applied to college nearly thirty years ago. I can't think of another time in my adult life when I've carved out this much of my day for something I created. And I may never again.

Prioritizing yourself is *fackin'* hard! You gotta give a shit about whether ya live or die! You have to say what you want and not keep it tucked away with all your other petty resentments. You have to deal with the troubling thought of people not being so hot about the idea that you're done being such a beta.

Yeah, that part.

Friends hate when friends change and start glowing up. And, in part, I know that's why I never prioritized myself. As the middle child, I don't like to ruffle feathers. I am the peacekeeper. Keeping the peace keeps me safe. But what happens when you've dimmed your light so much in every relationship or with every acquaintance you have that you forget who you are?

By doing so, you legitimately hazard your own sense of self, to say nothing of your health. To me, advocating and campaigning for yourself and your needs is the ultimate form of self-love. No shade, but please miss me with the caviar facials. All the manicures and red wine baths in the world will not save you the way a colon screening can. And, finally, I do not want to make this a binary proposition—that you can't have your jollies and indulgences too. Have your jollies! Take your indulgences! But at least put on your oxygen mask before you put on your Goop-ass bird poop face mask! As I said in Chapter 2, take care of yourself! Do you! Not to freak you out, but your life just might depend on it. 'Cause no amount of beeswax skin firmer is going to detect that growing polyp in your duff.

JUST THE TIPS, PLEASE

- **Tough self-love:** Real self-love is not about indulgence or decadence. It's about showing up for yourself in the baseline, boring tasks of life, like physicals and routine checkups.
- **Performative self-care = *No bueno*:** The culture of wellness and self-care has been hijacked by consumerism tailor-made for creating enviable displays on social media.
- **Ain't got time to bleed:** Oh but you do. Do not listen to Jesse "The Body" / "The Mind." Real men take care of themselves.

Chapter 8

CARL WINSLOW IS FULL OF SHIT AND TWINKIES

(And Other Things Your Teacher Never Taught You)

Do not go gentle into that good night,
Old age should burn and rave at close of day;
Rage, rage against the dying of the light.

—Dylan Thomas, "Do Not Go Gentle into That Good Night" (emphasis added)

IF YOU WANT TO STAY MARRIED, WORK OUT.

Let me be clear here and not misquoted. If you want to stay married, work out. Maybe you're wondering why you need to work out to stay married. I mean, the anecdotal evidence suggests that in our society, all a man needs is money and looks that at the very least do not induce vomiting. For Chrissakes, look at Harvey Weinstein! The guy has a face like a mile of bad road and a body like a sack-o-goo *and a gross gherkin-looking gherkin... allegedly!* And, yes, I just body-shamed convicted predator-man Harvey Weinstein. But if we can't roast him, we're officially too woke to function.

Anyway, like the vast majority of other cis, straight dudes in this country, I don't have Harvey Weinstein money. And if you look around, Americans have kinda been duped into thinking the proper body type for a married guy (prosperous or otherwise) is rotund like one Frederick Joseph W. Flintstone.

When I think of all the TV dads I grew up watching—Phil Banks, Carl Winslow, Dan from *Roseanne*, Homer Simpson, *that one that rhymes with "Shmosby"*—all of the dads were a little paunchy and a little out of shape, if not dangerously corpulent. These body types were *modeled* for us—out of shape, low energy, past their prime. That marked you as a husband. And just so long as you were able to provide, it didn't matter if you had a paunch or that you'd gotten gout for the second time in a year like your name is Henry VIII. But the way I see it, not many of us are sitcom dads, and we certainly aren't billionaires, but we do walk around like we are, with our flaccid, flimsy, bloated-ass bodies. We didn't invent the Tesla! I didn't dream up Amazon! I don't have billions to make me pop like an accent wall!

Let's really look at the images we've been sold in popular culture about what a dad is supposed to look like (tubby / on the couch) and recognize the impact they might have on how we carry ourselves.

NOT LOOKING LIKE A TUB OF SHIT HAS ITS BENEFITS

In the previous chapter, I discussed self-love—deep, trenchant, bottom-of-the-Mariana-Trench self-love. And now it's time to do a table flip because I'm going to let you in on a little secret that no one wants to talk about...one that I only recently discovered.

I haven't really exercised since I was in high school, and I only did that because my coaches made us. I was never really a fan of gym culture, and I would always tell myself that, because I lived in New York, all the walking, and running and sprinting (for various reasons, most bad), would be my gym. But right about the time I began writing this book, I started going for it. I went from a few days a week to no rest days (don't act like you're not impressed).

Here's what I have to tell you:

People treat you differently when you work out this much.

There. There's the secret. It's taboo to say and definitely off-menu at In-N-Out Burger, so to speak, but—fuck it! I've done the work and possess the receipts—loving yourself gets that much easier when people like what they're looking at. This is gross, I know, I *know*, but I remind you that the visual cortex occupies, like, 20 to 25 percent of the brain—a quarter of brain space. We can all strive to be our best selves (or whatever), but even we submit to the categorical natures of ourselves. It is what it is.

Now, I have always endeavored to maintain a healthy self-image and high self-esteem, but only recently did I realize that for much of my life, I was fighting with one hand tied behind my back. We have been encouraged by so many Dove soap commercials to love our bodies and that, in so doing, we will radiate a vibration so high that it will render us irresistible. I tried it. It didn't work (for me). Or that is to say, for me at least, it doesn't last.

Let's be honest, guys, it's hard to gin up that kind of equanimity as a middle-aged man by embracing what shows up in the mirror day after day. My brain is too jammed with doubts, fears, regrets, and petty jealousies. When I was a kid, my major worry was whether I'd ever be tall. It took up a lot of real estate. Luckily for me, and perhaps *because* of my fretting, kvetching, and kvelling (sorry, Dallas, I've been in NYC too long), I made it all the way to five foot ten (yes, they do stack shit that high). But that was my "major" worry as a kid. I didn't love my height, and I wasn't happy about it either.

When I became an adolescent, my bodily wants changed. I wanted a strong frame. I wanted to be cut from wood and shredded like a julienne salad, but I was turned off by what it took to achieve that kind of body. Let's be clear here: At a certain age (fifteen), a primary concern of mine (the only one, really) was attracting the female gaze. But since I wasn't blessed with the body of an Adonis or the face of Idris Elba on his worst day, I had to rely on my wit, my personality (yikes!), and—at least until recently—my lightning-quick metabolism. But then, as the years rolled by, my metabolism slowed to a crawl, and suddenly I was thick. Not the good "thicc," but *thick*—sweating from just standing around, shifting my weight from one foot to the next, perspiring around my beltline thick. Not fun. I knew I didn't like carrying around this extra weight or all the new wonderful sounds that accompany middle age—the groaning and huffing every time I got in and out of a seat, the random pains that come from just . . . *being*.

Like a lot of things, I shrugged it off as the cycle of life. There is nothing we can do about the irreversible Bataan Death March to the grave, right, kids? And since I was a Gen X latchkey kid, whenever I worried about my swelling thighs or my blooming love handles, I would reassure myself that I was merely becoming like one of the dads I saw so much on TV as a kid. I wasn't getting fat, I would tell myself. I was just coming into my final form—like a pudgy butterfly. This was my dad-bod era! My body was just marking itself as a dad. So, have another order of chicken wings with blue cheese dressing; have another ice cream even though you've had ice cream for literally three days in a row. Yeah! It's what you do when you're on the dad-bod diet. You're still a decent provider and quick with a joke. So what if you're sliding precariously into life-threatening obesity, right? Again, the TV told me I could still be a sack of decaying shit and also be happily married.

Growing up, the message was clear: Men of a certain age have it all and beer bellies.

I don't know who spread this myth, or seeded it so deeply in little boys' brains, but I am not ruling out Frederick Joseph W. Flintstone—"Fred," as he's known to his neighbor/coworker Barney Rubble. Fred, of course, was married to Wilma, his long-suffering wife who not only cooked her man savory Brontosaurus Burgers and Raptor Ribs but also looked like a whole snack doing it. Unlike Fred, Wilma was slim and healthy, and she never got on Fred about how much he ate, unless the writers were desperate for a story idea, I suppose. As I recall, Dad getting *too* overweight was an all-too-common trope in nineties sitcoms. Dad's weight was trotted out as a handy joke device. Dad's declining strength and failing health are a fun way to show the character's best days are behind him. Let's have a laugh at his hardening arteries, everybody! And, look, don't get me wrong. The shit is funny! But plenty of things are funny and wrong as hell. That's the beauty of comedy. However, there's serious side effects to that coin. Namely, prolonged obesity can lead to other comorbidities and, eventually, theoretically preventable death: *hahahaaaaaa...yeah....* Sorry to say the quiet part.

Point is, even outside the doctor saying my body is alive once a year—I'm much happier in shape than I was when my shape resembled something akin to a pear. Back then, my back always hurt. I had trouble getting up. I had trouble bending down. I was constantly looking for places to sit in public. I had trouble reaching things in high places. I had trouble carrying heavy shit. I had trouble carrying things that weren't so much heavy as they were unwieldy. I broke out in a sweat from doing absolutely nothing. I remember standing in a long line once, and my knee just popped (from the unbearable weight of my frame, I suppose). Sometimes I would just wake up in the morning and it felt like my ankles decided to work from home without telling me. If I wasn't in outright pain, I was living with a certain amount of constant discomfort. My shoulders hurt and I would get painful stitches in my chest, too.

In short, I was falling the fuck apart. And worse, nothing fit me anymore.

My thighs had grown so much that I was constantly threatening to split my pants like my name was Bruce Banner! Look, I know that all of us must make peace with our bodies, and at a certain point, I was confronted with buying clothes that were actually in my size. I was going to have to embrace the fact that, in my forties, this was just who I was. I was nearly thirty pounds heavier than what my driver's license said and I had pretty luscious thighs (which is great if that's what you're into). And I guess that was yet another watershed moment for me. When I was faced with buying a whole new wardrobe to accommodate my bigger frame, I didn't. Why?

Because I was going to turn my life around?

Not so much. I'm just cheap.

Yeah, I wish I had a better answer for you, dear reader, but I don't spend a lot of money on clothes as it is. I am doing my part not to contribute to the horrors of fast fashion, y'all.

Just kidding! Again, I'm just a cheap dude! But being cheap has its perks, namely, not buying a ton of clothes that eventually end up in the Pacific Gyre. Call me *Captain Planet*, everybody!

So yeah, that was my inflection point. Either I go up a size aka spend more coins *or* get in shape and spend nothing. I chose the latter.

Of course, the road to working out seven days a week (which is not for everyone, obviously) wasn't easy.

It's 5:00 a.m. wakeups. It's blood, sweat, tears, and dry heaves. It's liquifying kale, and feeling pain in places you have to find in *Gray's Anatomy* (the book, not the show). Other than fitting back in my clothes and staving off spending on newer, bigger threads, I didn't have much of a goal in mind. Then, goals started to reveal themselves. New York can be a veritable gauntlet of stressful environments. There are endless stairs, crowds, total characters, cars, semis, buses, and too much to list here. It's hard to survive here if you sit around all day like a pasha. You gotta move. And that's out of home.

SCHLEPPING

I learned this word when I moved to New York. *Schlep* is one of those Yiddish words that is used universally among

New Yorkers. It means "to lug," but it has a wonderful spank of onomatopoeia. On any given day in my home there is so much to be schlepped—groceries, laundry (dirty, clean, and somewhere in between), trash, recycling, compost, et cetera. TP and PT need restocking. Dishes need to be put away (after they're cleaned and dried, of course—learned that the hard way!). Also, finicky flowers need watering, the fridge needs to be stocked, and food must be cooked. The beds need stripping. The beds need to be made. The dog needs to be fed. The dog needs to be walked. Where is the dog? On and on and on, ad infinitum.

The unending chores and details churn on with the steady drumbeat of domesticity. It seems like a lot because it is indeed a lot. Just to do these tasks, think of all of the ways the body must twist, contort, bend, and reach daily. When I consider it, it makes me want to win the Powerball and hire an army of servants. Absent that very unlikely scenario, here we all are.

I want to be very clear here. I don't enjoy doing chores any more than I ever did. But I've now eliminated one of the *major reasons* why I don't like doing chores—because they are hard on my body.

Now, they aren't.

I have a couple of male relatives who sport serious bellies. Whenever their partners ask them to do something that would require them to get off the couch, it's a problem. And my male relatives (tryna keep names out of it) always seem to get that much more cross because they look like expectant mamas in their third trimester trying to rise from the sectional whenever Wifey calls. There is a palpable vexation. Getting up is that much harder when you're carrying excess weight around your waist and thighs. You start making weird-ass grunts akin to a stressed/pressed water buffalo to encourage rising, and you really start depending on your arms, maybe pitching yourself forward and back and hoping to achieve some kind of momentum. It's a lot.

But here's the thing: Even if I am holding it down around the house and doing my utmost, invariably there are bound to be oversights, and if I am sitting on the couch minding my own (something Wife abhors), there's a good chance I will be asked to do something that requires getting off my chocolate rump. But then, like a scene out of the classic *Karate Kid* training montage, there was a breakthrough. Suddenly, I made a connection between my workouts in my basement and my newfound inclination toward housework.

Quite by accident I dusted off my kettlebell and started swinging that bad boy three or four times per week. I did goblet squats and swing-to-squats and lunges and Bulgarian squats and Romanian deadlifts. (Real quick: Can we address that any exercise that comes out of the former Soviet Union is pure, unalloyed torture?)

Anyway, I went in on these workouts, and suddenly my hip flexors, quads, hamstrings, core, and posterior chain came online. And if we've been following along, those muscles do most of the heavy lifting involved in lifting your heavy ass off the couch. Suddenly, I could lift myself out of a deep-ass Adirondack chair like it was my job. And if Wifey needed something that required my particular set of skills, at least getting up to do it wasn't an additional chore. Nothing was going to be harder than my final set of predawn one-legged rows.

Something else I love about my cheapo workout regimen is the effect it has on my mental health. It took a long, long time (maybe too long), but I now enjoy very prolonged runner's highs that can last hours on end—and I'm telling you, you can too. Hear me out, because I remember exactly when this first happened.

Let me first say that I love an edible. You can't smoke everywhere and I am one of the few people who can operate on edibles (at least I *think* I can). *Did you hear something different?!* Anyway, recently one morning I was sitting down to write. I had done my daily morning torture session of kettlebell swings and cardio, and now it was time to go to the literary salt mines to hammer away at another chapter. Sentence upon grueling sentence, I prayed to the gods of cogency and coherence. I don't always feel this way about writing, but more often than not, my process (LOL) comes with a certain amount of ennui. And since I live in New York, I have just accepted that as coin of the realm.

And trust me, I know what I sound like—I live in NYC and you don't, so suck it! But before you come for the coastal elites doing coastal elite shit, let me admit that all New Yorkers, it seems, are a little sad, a little tired, and a little sick. But that day I felt a little weird. Strangely, I wasn't reflexively checking Instagram to see how my latest dumb post did. I wasn't googling myself or jumping down headline holes about world issues I am powerless to control. Instead, I was just typing away. *What edible did I take?* I thought. *Was it that new one I'd scored at that spot in the Berkshires?* Then it hit me. I had skipped the edible that day, and I don't drink coffee.

Oh shit! Was I having a stroke?! Were these my final moments? I smell toast!

I was only on season 1 of *House of the Dragon*, though.... *Quel dommage*. Turns out, it was just something I hadn't felt (clothes on) since I was a kid—euphoria. This was a prolonged, sustained euphoria brought on by, well,... *me!* High on this crest of well-being, I made light work of my writing for the day. The next day was the same, and the day after that, too. Of course, I don't get a prolonged endorphin rush *every* day, but it is happening more often than not. I love that it comes from me. I love that it was completely unexpected. Prolonged endorphin and cannabinoid highs are akin to finding twenty dollars in your jacket pocket on the first day of winter. You did not see it coming, but you are definitely not mad about it. And here's another plus: Runner's highs—at least in my experience—are hard to upset. Recently, things that would otherwise annoy me—chatter, tasks, deadlines—seem that much more bearable, and getting off the couch to do something for my family seems less odious.

So the question remains: Do you need to work out every day to save your marriage? I think you already know the answer is no (unless you are avenging the death of your family at the hands of Ra's al Ghul and the Legion of Shadows). But, friend, you *need* to move. It's time. It's time to design your own watershed and eliminate one of the factors that makes helping out difficult.

While you think it over, here's another wonderful aspect of getting active. Oof, when we reach our forties, we're no longer exercising, we're "staying active"—as though I'm doing Jazzercise at the area senior center. But staying *active* not only boosts your mood and your circulation, but for me at least, it also meant the end of my ED prescription. Yahtzee! It's better on the other side, folks. Now I don't have to remember to take a pill. I just have to remember to set my alarm for my morning workout. And, yes, in case you were wondering, sex is that much better. In my case, it's the best it's ever been. That's one way to chase away the relationship *mehs.* And here's another fun aspect. Now Wifey and I can actually do most of those positions that I've seen the professionals do *and* our sex lasts for a longer time, too.

At first I thought it was a fluke, but now I am convinced. *Choreplay* handily rhymes with *foreplay*, but Holy Hump Day does it work! We are all adults here, so I will just say that prior to my health journey, holding myself up in the missionary position came with shaky arms, but now that's not a thing.

I don't worry about when my back or shoulders are going to give out. They don't. I don't worry if my hips are going to full on go into dysplasia, either. They don't. And I no longer worry about the wobbles if we are doing it in the style of the dog. Until I started working out regularly, sex had been restricted to a few positions, and now I'd say that Wife and I have added a few more. We aren't at Kama Sutra levels, of course, as some things remain prohibited in certain states, but here's hoping!

In sum, I don't feel like shit anymore and I don't look like it either. My body feels strong and healthy. My back doesn't hurt from sitting in chairs or standing in lines. I feel sturdy. I feel solid. I feel healthy. I could also get fully taken out by a bus that can't drop below 50 mph tomorrow, but still!

GAME PLAN

So how do you get like me?

I don't know if you have what it takes (you definitely do). And I am barely a professional comedian and definitely not a professional trainer. But suffice it to say, I will share my workout regimen with you. Consult with an actual health and fitness professional if you are looking to get annoyingly serious. First, let me tell you that my routine has evolved into something super simple but effective.

Here it is.

A REASONABLE, REPEATABLE, REAL-PERSON WORKOUT PLAN

(OR: HOW TO MOVE YOUR BODY WITHOUT JOINING A CULT OR RUINING YOUR KNEES)

Monday

Yoga Sculpt

Kick off the week strong with a yoga sculpt class or video. It's like yoga's jacked cousin—squats, curls, and planks hiding inside sun salutations. You'll sweat, maybe swear, but feel like a champ by the end.

Tuesday

Walk + Kettlebell Mini-Circuit

30-minute brisk walk (solo, podcast, or pet-friendly)

3 rounds of:

- 12 kettlebell swings
- 10 goblet squats
- 8 bent-over rows (each arm)
- 30 seconds of plank
- **Bonus:** Try not to drop the kettlebell on your foot. It's bad for morale.

Wednesday

Yoga Sculpt or Restorative Stretch

If you're sore, opt for a chill stretchy yoga session.

If you're not, go sculpt again and give those glutes the where- and what for.

Thursday

Kettlebell Flow + Core Work

3 rounds of:

- 10 kettlebell deadlifts
- 10 alternating reverse lunges with kettlebell pass-through
- 10 kettlebell push presses (5 each side)

Finish with:

- 30 bicycle crunches
- 20 Russian twists (with or without weight)
- 1-minute side plank (30 seconds each side)

Friday

Yoga Sculpt

Your end-of-week sweat. Think of it as earning your weekend wine or the ability to collapse on the couch without guilt.

Saturday

Vinyasa Yoga

Time to chill. Flow it out. No weights, no lunges, just a nice reminder you do, in fact, still have hamstrings.

Sunday

Optional Rest or "Whatever Moves You" Day

Walk. Twerk in your kitchen. Foam roll. Chase your kid. Clean the garage like you're training for *American Ninja Warrior*. Or rest. You earned it.

What I like about this plan is that it's really just two different exercises, yoga and kettlebells: One day you're lifting heavy and the next you're stretching out those same muscles that you just worked. I can tell you that one makes the other that much easier to do. The more I swing my kettlebell, the easier it becomes to balance on one leg or pull off a headstand. And the more skandasanas (half squats) I put in, the easier it becomes to do my goblet squats and/or one-leg deadlifts. One discipline supports the other, and I am more than satisfied with the results. I have to admit that I don't take rest days because that's just my brand, and it's not like these are three-hour-long gym rotations every day. I'm just either all in or definitely not. In my life I've struggled to commit. Never did I ever think that something I would commit to would be fitness.

If you're just starting off, go slow, but do start off!

PRO TIP: DO IT AT HOME

I'd suggest compiling your own little home gym. Since you're buying the equipment, in the long run it will always cost less than paying gym fees monthly. And, really, it doesn't take all that much to get started. My entire gym setup includes my yoga mat, my yoga block, a set of ten-pound dumbbells that belong to my wife, and a pair of kettlebells—twenty pounds and thirty pounds, respectively. If you work out at home in a space with no mirrors, it's that much easier to eliminate judgments and stave off comparisons that you might otherwise be making at the gym.

ANOTHER PRO TIP: GET UP EARLY

One of the biggest obstacles to staying active is remaining consistent. To do that while meeting the challenge of my responsibilities as a partner and a parent, I had to find a workaround.

In the before times, before I choreplayed/raptured, I would try to get in a workout in the morning after I had dropped off the kids at school or before dinner. That was a big nerp because I was constantly being interrupted by emails, texts, or tasks. Or my kids would want to play in the same space where I was exercising and I would get all huffy until they walked away, crestfallen that their dad was such a salty ogre. On a very good friend's advice, I tried something radical, and perhaps the single most radical thing I would advise anyone do for choreplay: I woke up early.

I am an unrepentant night owl. Without coffee, I can stay up until three in the morning. Yeah, I'm a real dirtbag. Thanks to years of late-night stand-up comedy gigs, I have the body clock of a Vietnam War–era grunt. And even though I never thought it possible, I flipped this paradigm. I willed myself to be a morning person. It's not easy to wake up as early as I do (4:45 a.m. or 5:00 a.m.), but it's kinda amazing. The house is completely silent and I have all the time I want to devote to exercise. I can take my time and set up my mat. I can find the right YouTube video. I can get the water bottle I like. I can get a nice fluffy towel and throw on a good workout set (outfit). And when I am done I can shower, eat, or catch up on a show (in silence!).

I would be remiss not to tell you that morning people bug me to distraction. I resent their superior bearing, but I will give them this. If you want to win the day, get up before the sun. Recently, I have been attending predawn yoga sculpt and predawn workout classes in Manhattan. Here's what I can tell you. The Patrick Batemans of the world are up before dawn, and pushing themselves to optimal physical condition. These people do not play. And though I do not care for their slavish devotion to capitalism, I will give them this: Bateman types know how to create an edge for themselves. I'm happy to emulate that. Also, don't trust Patrick Bateman types with an ax, especially if they're wearing a see-through raincoat and listening to eighties pop in their living room. If you know, you know....

DIET

Picasso said that kids are the best artists because they know when their creation is done. That is, they know when to leave the table. That said, I am not here to push some crash diet on you. In fact, I'll submit that what I eat is not going to get you into some kind of fat-free, fighting shape, but what it has done has made me feel much better. So, since we're out here chorin' and playin' and whatnot, and this book is about solidarity (not telling you what to do or what to eat, and never telling you how to feel!), here is what I eat in a typical day. Note: I do not count calories because, despite the fact that I do wear glasses, I'm not much of a mathlete, and if you don't eat over-processed slop, there's no need.

Breakfast

Oatmeal (organic rolled oats)—I typically make myself one bowl with a pat of butter, cinnamon (for inflammation), Craisins, raisins, or blueberries as well as a dollop of maple syrup because, otherwise, gross. Or breakfast is granola and prolly an apple with whole milk for me (very exciting, I know!). And if I'm doing that, it's two soft-boiled eggs with salt, pepper, and olive oil with a side of avocado. And on Sundays, I cheat and have a bacon-egg-and-cheese or pancakes or pastries or bagels and their brother from another mother, lox. In short, Sunday is when I eat all the garbage I've really been wanting to eat all week.

Lunch

Smoothie time. I am a middle-aged man trying to keep his broken-down jalopy body on the road of life. Of course I sip on smoothies! The things in my smoothie I would likely not eat on their own unless they were rendered into liquid first. But typically my smoothies consist of the following:

- Ice
- Water (are you with me so far?)
- Bananas, for something sweet
- Watercress*
- At least 4 dates (pitted, 'cause otherwise, yikes!)
- Blueberries
- Turmeric
- Ginger
- Greek yogurt

Dinner

Mostly, I eat whatever my family is eating. I don't want to be that guy who brings his own food to the party. I'm also not training for the decathlon right now (or ever), so this is the meal where I go in. In a typical week, though, I'd say my family and I eat salmon, chicken, lots of pasta (we're in NYC), and then go out for dinner on the weekends. We are also very lucky in that my mother-in-law is a gourmand and lives right around the corner, so we enjoy at least one fancy home-cooked meal per week.

I typically don't turn down dessert when it's offered, and since I am a social drinker and New Yorkers are hella pushy, I

---

* I cannot say enough about watercress. It's a superfood that is supercheap. It's packed with vitamin C, and sidenote: It's a super-affordable natural Viagra. I kept ingesting it and soon enough things downstairs were back with a vengeance.

have a glass of wine or two with dinner when I go to eat at my mother-in-law's place. So, basically, dinner is my time to treat myself a little—a little vino, a little ice cream here and there. When it comes to junk and vice, my MO is to pepper, don't pour.

And then there are just foods that I've kind of "left on read," so to speak. Like, I don't eat a lot of steak anymore (sad). I try not to eat candy unless it's Halloween. I eat hamburgers and hot dogs only between Memorial Day and Labor Day ('Murica). I don't drink soda or beer all that much either. It kills me to say it, but I hear all these foods are reportedly doing pretty well without me. Sometimes it sucks a golf ball through a garden hose to eat this way, but the green juice is worth the squeeze. I rarely if ever get headaches. I don't have stomach issues either. Yes, I know you were wondering, so I'll tell you. I am *muy muy* regular (this brings us that much closer).

On this subject of diet, at least, I'm not saying you have to do what I do. I'm sure a lot of you will tell me I'm doing it wrong. If so, feel free to have thoughts. What I am saying is that we likely need to look somewhere other than beloved TV dads when it comes to body norms.

I mean, look, I'm not a sociologist. Again, I am just a simple comedian who makes his living trying to write the occasional elevated "men be doing this" and "women be doing that" joke. Can I prove a link between the epidemic of male obesity in this country and one Fred Flintstone? I can do my best! Yep, the TED Talk is inbound and not to be missed. In the meantime, allow me to proffer that, despite our cognitive dissonance on the topic, in America at least, the majority of us are reared on screens of one kind or another. The screens provide us with stories. They teach us right from wrong. They suggest what to like and give us our opinions. They tell us how to look. How to speak. And how to be. That said, I'm confident enough to argue that there is a correlation between the myriad images I've been fed of the over-the-hill middle-aged yutz and my slow slide into elevated BMI. In short, on a long enough timeline, you become what you behold.

Listen, one of my biggest pet peeves in any discussion is when folks try to isolate a single root cause of an issue as complex as obesity. That gumbo's got a lot simmering in it—government subsidies for corn syrup and fast food, the explosion of video games and social media—they've all got a hand in the mix. As we've said for my generation, the core memories of what a dad looks like can be traced back to TV. For Gen X, television was our babysitter and our teacher. It never judged us and passed down so many chestnuts during the very special episodes. Can it really be all that surprising that three out of every four red-blooded American males resemble network TV dads from the eighties? Yep, according to the CDC, 75 percent of men born between 1965 and 1980 (Gen X) are overweight or obese. In fact, Gen X males beat the national average (74 percent) by a percentage point. Suck it, boomers!

Let me conclude by saying that while I was growing up my father wasn't always around. He was busy delivering babies and saving lives or whatever. But he thrives in his seventies (cat's out of the bag), clocking in daily six-mile walks, rain or shine. It's admirable and a reminder that, as beloved as they might be (deep breath!), *sometimes* our TV fathers fail us. That's a lot to process, I know.

Now, somebody pass me a hoagie. This writing shit can make a brother hungry!

Chapter 9

GO THE F**K TO SLEEP, YOU SLEEPLESS F**K

I AM AWARE I SPENT A WHOLE-ASS CHAPTER TELLING YOU THAT I am a newly minted morning person, but let me also reiterate that I do not care for morning people. I'm not finished dunking on these pre-dawn-douchers. Morning people are a smug sort. They tell you the litany of things that they accomplished while you—an obvious slob—were still drooling on your pillow. Their toxic air of superiority and imperious swagger can definitely give off *American Psycho* / social Darwinism vibes. Because, as they'll so happily tell you, as you slept, they rose early for a bracing predawn workout (they led the class). They finished that book (as in, finished writing it). They made a breakthrough in their cancer research, which they do for funzies. They swung by a farmers market for the freshest produce but only *after* scaling El Capitan. Then, they hit up the *boulangerie* for the freshest breads, but not before placing a baby osprey back in its nest. They somehow also found time to have a spa day with their friends from college and cook a gourmet catch-up breakfast for their parents, with whom they hadn't spoken in twelve years. They rescued a dog, but it also rescued them! And they did all this before you woke up, ya sleepyhead.

That said, research shows that morning people do tend to outperform their night-owl counterparts in various aspects of life. A study by biologist Christoph Randler found that early risers are more proactive and more likely to anticipate problems and minimize them, leading to higher levels of success.[1] And, of course, morning people need night owls like me. We make them feel better about themselves by comparison. And unless they're writing their magnum opus by candlelight, night-owl people don't have all that much to brag about. I'm willing to bet that night people would just as soon forget their nocturnal exploits rather than share them. So, does that mean you have to become a morning person to truly achieve fullest choreplay? What it means is you need to get your ass up early but don't have to be a horse's ass about it. Keep that shit to yourself.

As a comic, I am a child of the night. The majority of comedy shows happen at night, often pushing into the wee hours of the morning, so comedy is ideal for me and my love of all things after-hours. Throughout my marriage, comedy has been the perfect excuse to stay out till 2:00 a.m. even though I had to take my kids to school the next morning. Like my dad before me, I'd found the cheat codes to stay out and up with justification. Except my dad was a doctor and I am a guy who entertains people on doomed online dates. But can you blame me for wanting to get my fill of NYC by night? If you've never been, let me just say—on the right night, the city is nothing less than an overwhelming spectacle of sound and fury. The bright lights and attractions enchant and seduce. It pulsates and pounds with possibility and adventure. Who could sleep through that?!

While I was growing up, my parents were very strict about bedtime. If they caught us out of bed, let's just say they would bring the MMA energy. And the more they punished me, the more I wanted to stay up.

I wanted to watch all the "grown folks" movies my dad was watching. After lights out, I would slither on my belly from my room on the far side of the house, through the sunken living room (where you weren't allowed to hang out 'cause it was for guests), past the dining room, and across the cold tile of the kitchen until finally arriving in the TV room on cat's paws. I would squeeze my nimble little frame along the back of the couch and try not to make a sound as my dad threw on the finest in Man Cinema—*Goodfellas, Unforgiven, Raging Bull, Death Wish, The Untouchables,* and the like—exactly what a young, impressionable boy should be watching. My dad has a penchant for gangster movies and westerns. He spent so much time sewing people up at the hospital that I think he kind of enjoyed watching them being blown to bits for his amusement.

So late nights were my rebellion, too. No one was going to tell me when to go to bed (actually, they totally were, but still!).

Like Dad, I was going to stay up and thumb my nose at convention and good health. Besides, the Disney Channel's offerings couldn't hold a candle to *Cape Fear*! And the work of auteurs like Spike Lee, Tarantino, Michael Mann, and Terrence Malick likely wasn't going to be playing right after *Double Dare*.

As Mark Twain said, "History doesn't always repeat itself, but it often rhymes."[2] My father's nocturnal restlessness did not come from the same angst as mine—he saved lives, I make jokes—but just the same, it came from angst. It came from wanting some modicum of control in one's life, no matter how trivial, even if it meant risking good health and, in my case at least (can't speak for Dad), my marriage too.

When I started to put the work in to revamp my marriage, I knew one of the major keys was fixing bedtime. Let's just say, Wifey and I go to bed at different times. She prefers to be in bed by nine o'clock (she's a monster!), and even on nights when I wasn't out doing stand-up comedy, I would often join her a little later around... ohhhhh, 2:00 or 2:30 a.m. (because I'm Nosferatu, apparently!). I did this every night for years. So on top of the time we were apart at our jobs, we were also apart for another 5.5 hours. Mathing the math here: 5.5 × 365 days = 2,007.5 hours, or 83.6 days, apart from one another yearly. In a given year, that means we spent nearly two out of every five days apart from one another. No wonder we weren't connecting.

Unlike me, Wife struggles to sleep. Not only is she more anxious than I am (she's a native New Yorker), but she's also negotiating all the trials that come with both her cycle and perimenopause, too. All that to say, sleep isn't always easy for her. For years she would call out to me in the night to come to bed or venture downstairs at ungodly hours to find me passed out on the couch to bring me to bed. Jerk that I am, whenever Wife complained about my late-night habits, I scoffed and diminished her very valid concerns. It wasn't unreasonable for her to want me to be in bed with her late at night. What in the gaslight was I doing? Did I get away with this behavior for way too long? Yes. Am I proud of it? ~~Yes.~~ No, but I did enjoy watching the "Battle of the Bastards" episode of *GOT* over and over again.

Now would be a good time to tell you that what we not gonna do is sit here and try to convince you with facts and figures about how sleep is good for you (it is), and how it can improve memory, stave off dementia, tune up the immune system, and increase mental health. So, instead, I will confine my remarks here to sleep as it relates to relationship health. Allow me to just cut to the chase and say that taking my dumbass to bed may have done the absolute most to save my *blah* marriage.

Sleep is a very hot topic these days. Everyone I know seems unable to get a good night's rest as of late. But then there is *a lot* going on (global warming, fraught elections, Taylor Swift, Ukraine, AI, Gaza, Joey Chestnut, to name a few), and it seems borderline impossible to hold the demons at bay long enough to get that sweet, sweet REM sleep. Lucky for me and my marriage, I can sleep anywhere anytime, and I have. I can sleep in the back of Ubers and on subways. I can sleep in waiting rooms. I can sleep at parties. I can sleep in meetings. I can sleep on Zooms. I can sleep at airport gates, too (not recommended because of the whole "miss your flight" thang). I even nod off while driving. What a fun party trick! Bottom of the bottom line: If there is sleep to be had, I am partaking. Another thing to add to my list of soft skills on LinkedIn (kidding).

My keen ability to just close my eyes and sleep for hours on end can drive Wife up a wall. She'll tell me how she woke up in the night, and tongue well in cheek, I'll ask, "What was I doing during all this?" I don't expect an answer. I should expect a forearm shiver. One look from her is answer enough, though. Suffice it to say, your manz can sleep! And if you're a sleepy slob like me, repairing the tatters of your relationship may well be within your grasp (provided you don't snore!).

As I stated earlier, sleep was and was not a problem for me. I *can* sleep. Once I close my eyes and cut the lights, I'm off to the races. For me, it's more a matter of unresolved id. The child in me wants to stay up like the grown-ups do!

But lucky for me, the pandemic came along.

Thanks to COVID-19 (said no one ever), stand-up comedy shows suddenly stopped altogether. That definitely kept me in the house, as we all know. Then, horror, it was too risky for some of my favorite networks and studios—HBO, Netflix, C-SPAN 2—to make new content for a while. Yikes! I wish I could tell you that I started to go to bed earlier because I wanted to be intentional and proactive, but that simply was not the case. As usual, I fell in shit. It is my brand and, as Desus and Mero would say, "The brand is strong."

With no new dumb reality shows or prestige dramas to watch and nowhere to be, I took a leap and did what I recommend you all do. *I went to bed when my partner went to bed* (*!!!*)... WOW! I know. What year is it?! I have dropped nothing but new-age truth bombs programmed to scramble your gray matter throughout the entirety of this book. But let me just say, sometimes I do what my partner does because on some things (all things), they know best. Of course, when I decided to show up for bedtime with Wife, it was... a little weird. She definitely had questions. She asked if I felt sick. She asked if I was feeling depressed or fatigued. The answer was no to all of the above, but her questions spoke to something larger.

We were out of sync and had been for years—we hadn't had the same bedtime since we'd moved in together. I chafed at the fact that my person woke up early for her job as a high school history teacher. I didn't like the rigor in that, that come what may she was in bed on time because that's what the job required. To rebel, I would sneak out of bed and, much like I did as a kid, would quietly tiptoe down the hall to watch hours of late-night TV. Oy, someone please page Dr. Freud because I realize now that my late-night TV sessions were just evidence of a child growing older and more distant from their person. Fortunately, I'm on the other side of it now. If I do a stand-up show, I'm generally back around ten o'clock or so, and I don't really stay up late to watch TV all that much, either.

Suffice it to say, I can't really advise you on *how* to go to bed. What part of "not a sleep expert" is unclear? I can say from experience, though, that it's in your best interest to go to bed, namely, for a reason I did not expect. The sex! Turns out, going to bed with my person eventually led to us having more intimate couple time which led to . . . the sex! Ever heard of it?! And another baby, you guys! *Just kidding!* Let's not speak that into existence.

Dad jokes to the side, I was shocked at how much more noodling we were getting up to. Sometimes it would be right after the kids had finally knocked off for the night. And sometimes it would be after she was done with some devastating article in *The New Yorker* about China's faceless masses. And then other times we'd get it all the way in at some odd hour in the dead of night when one or both of us woke up feeling like jumping junk-first into the bone zone (can you tell how comfortable I am talking about sex, y'all?). This was new! We weren't those kinda people, were we? Before I could even begin to answer that question, her retainer would come out and undies came off! Suddenly, we didn't care about each other's halitosis. Both of us were on it like a silk bonnet!

Fuck what you've heard. Cuddled up to your person seventeen years into a marriage—that's where ya wanna be!

I marvel at how much of my journey back to my person went through shutting our eyes at the same damn time. Sure, we had gone to therapy throughout the years, and we had made real efforts to connect via date nights and the like, but discovering getting into bed with my person at their appointed bedtime as the world experienced something of an apocalypse really did the trick! That said, please don't go about finding your way to your marriage bed exactly like I did, predicated by a pandemic. But if it can be helped, I suggest you get in there one way or the other. ESPN's programming is great and all, but it doesn't beat smashing! It also doesn't beat those wonderful late-night check-in hours I'd been missing these many years.

Wife and I had both been unwinding separately rather than with each other. We'd put the kids to bed, clean the dishes, and prepare for the day ahead, but we didn't power down *together*. I'd honestly forgotten how fortifying it can be to do just that. Wife is very good at padding down in her nest, so to speak. For some reason, I'd repressed my ability to do the same. I couldn't soothe myself without one sort of screen or another. I admire the way my wife puts on more comfortable clothes when she comes home for the day. I never made a habit of doing that. Growing up that just wasn't done in my house. You stayed in your outdoor clothes till you went to bed. I realize I've lost some of you here, but I guess that's what I get for putting myself out there! But when I began to go to bed with Wife, something just shifted. For too long I'd repressed so many other healthy bedtime impulses and urges. Turns out, I could go to bed at a decent hour, too. Wife didn't have a monopoly on the bedtime game.

And to my great surprise, I found out that I really liked our room, too. Until very recently, my kids would call our room

"Mom's room." That really says it all, doesn't it? Why would them kids lie, right?! You would think that would have given me pause, but willfully ignorant slob that I am sometimes, I let it slide. I'm happy to report, though, that these days the kids call our bedroom "Mom and Dad's room." And what a room it is!

We spent months picking out the wallpaper and all the appointments. We installed pocket doors in the closets and painstakingly hunted down the right tufted headboard. With its touches of marble and custom woodwork, if I'm being honest, I think I felt like the room didn't belong to me. In fact, I spent so little time in there that I didn't even realize that, at one point, my wife had removed the bulb from my bedside lamp. What did I need it for, right?

When I made my way back into our room, I started moving back in other ways, too. I rearranged my slovenly drawers and tidied up my side of the closet, too. Little by little, the clothes piles on my side of the bed receded like a melting glacier of funky-smelling hoodies, boxer briefs, and mismatched socks. Breakthrough incoming:

The more time I spend in *our* room, the more I respect the space.

Instead of treating our bedroom as a place to crash, I treated it as a place to decompress and unwind. Our overtaxed couch cushions couldn't be happier. Trust.

And, finally, in case I haven't made a strong enough argument as to why you should bed down at night with your mate, allow me to proffer two last points. First, when you go the fuck to sleep, you avoid the late-night drama of the snack variety.

When it comes to midnight snacks, I am a stan. I love my ice cream or my cereal or my leftover Thai or a yummy-ass tuna fish sammy! Who doesn't? And something else I liked to do in the before days was leave my bowls and glasses and cups and dishes and cutlery and other ephemera on the coffee table. Since I would go to bed so late, my wife would invariably find my detritus and a wake of debris from the night before, something that made her none too happy. Now, some might say I was leaving signs of passing so that my wife would know where I'd been (cute), but those people are lucky if they aren't involuntarily single for life. One way to avoid my habit of leaving out dishes is (you guessed it) going to bed when my partner does! Since I made this change, the incidents of dishes left out in the morning have plummeted, and since I wake up so early now, even if I do leave a dish out—oh snap!—I scoop that thing in the pale light of dawn, with my wife none the wiser.

That brings me to the final reason why going to bed with your person just makes sense.

Deep breath.

To be blunt, ain't nothing for you out there. As I've said, I've done the very unscientific research for you. Staying up as late as I did, did nothing to improve my marriage or my life, for that matter. Instead of connecting with my wife, I just watched

TV, stayed out drinking with my fellow comedians, watched stupid reality TV or, worse, watched professionals do sex, and/ or doomscrolled on IG (or both). What was I doing, though? What in the name of slow-moving self-destruction was I trying to prove?

Ever since I was a child I was drawn by the TV glow. I would hold my nose up close to the screen sometimes and let the static tickle it. Just me? OK…I was taken in by the stories and the fantasies of a world just beyond my reach. I took wicked pleasure in staying up past my bedtime to do it. I think I loved the transgressive element in that. But was it ever worth it to be a watcher? Was it ever worth it to be that much of a passive voyeur? Do I really need to answer these questions? And perhaps better questions to ask are, Why can't I let go of my fantasies? Why can't I let go of my need to act out? I don't have answers yet, but I do know this much: The more I go to bed with my person, the better it gets. I get to have the romantic interludes with my partner that I see on-screen. I get to be what I used to behold. *I* get the girl!

All it took was going the fuck to sleep!

JUST THE TIPS, PLEASE

Going to Bed, the Slob's Way

If you're staying up late and you're not a crypto bro or a software engineer putting the final touches on the source code that's going to upend the way we eat cucumbers or some other nonsense, harken unto me. These are a few of my best methods for getting effective shut-eye.

Edibles

How I go to sleep isn't exactly legal in all fifty states (I see you, Mississippi!). But when I have trouble winding down in general, I grab for a low-grade edible. Edibles are not for everyone (I prefer indica over sativa because I don't want to pay for my panic attacks). Also, make sure you are well enough to have one and that you keep the dosage lawful and low-fi.

Bedtime Reminder

Also, I set a reminder on my phone that tells me when to go to bed. I set that bad boy for 10:30 and then it goes off and I get cross and only then finally take my averse ass to bed around eleven. I highly recommend doing this. Its efficacy lies in its repetition. Sometimes I can anticipate that the reminder is going to ding moments before it does. I'm psychic, you guys.

Be a Little Toxic

Draft off of your person. Sometimes I try to go to bed *before* my mate and relish in their expression. The existential questions that this presents to my person are written all over their face. After all, how can she be the responsible one if I'm going to bed before her? Does not compute! Make it make sense. Nighty night!

Chapter 10

THE INCREDIBLE BULK

IN THE LAST FEW CHAPTERS, WE'VE TOUCHED ON PROPER DIET, exercise, and rest and what role these play in the ultimate chore of looking out for yourself. We're making serious strides, so I want to unbox a hack to save you time, effort, and even brain power, which always seems to elude me. My favorite part of this hack is that it can be done from your smartphone—no kettlebells or predawn shenanigans required. Yeah, over here in choreplay we pimp smarter, not harder. And since we covered exercise, let's dig into bulking up...on unsalted organic butter...I'll see myself out.

Quick story: The first time I had to cook for myself was the year my parents took me off my college meal plan. It's something that will live in infamy.

When my parents perpetrated this unspeakable act, I was responsible for (deep breath) *all* my meals! Yes, my parents were literal monsters. How did I fare? As you can likely guess, not well. I will never forget my first grocery run. Did I make a list? Pfft! Lists? Those were for moms and coupon-slanging grannies. Your man was going to shop by vibes alone. What did I get? What any red-blooded twenty-two-year-old male would get: Tostitos with a *hint* of lime, Tostitos queso "cheese product" dip, salsa (what? I'm from Texas!), bread, Ring Dings, ground chuck, bacon, an onion, and zero TP, fruits, veggies, deodorant (all musk!), or eggs.

Very self-sufficient, I know. It's not like my ne'er-do-well roommate was any help, though. Beyond the occasional onions and high-end cheese he'd pick up at a snooty specialty store, he ordered cheap takeout every night. As a newly minted adult, I was trying to keep a little jingle in my pocket. With that belief in my own adulting, I headed home from the fateful first "for us / by us" grocery run. I didn't have a car in college (cue: violins), so I had to (sigh) *carry* the bags all the way back to my apartment. The struggle was real.... But as I was crossing the quad, and in plain view of some very attractive classmates, I fully tripped over my own Adidas sliders and busted my whole butt. I went ass-over-teakettles. My bags flew up in the air and came crashing down in a shower of broken glass, salsa, gooey queso dip, and a few smartass cheers. Not cute. Ashamed to show my face again, I took all my classes remotely for the rest of the semester (kidding). But I was out here looking like Black Kevin McCallister back from his grocery run, when his shopping bags quit and his haul spilled all over his suburban Chicago sidewalk. PS, if you haven't seen *Home Alone* yet and I just spoiled it for you, I offer no apologies. You did this to yourself!

Because of this core memory and the untold thousands of times I sat through weekly grocery store runs with my parents, me and the groceries were not cool. I was able to dodge grocery duty for a super-long time. Even after Wife and I cohabitated and eventually married, your boy was never out here hunting for the ideal level of pulp in the Tropicana (the answer is always "some" pulp, by the way). In part, this was because Wife belonged to a crunchy Brooklyn food co-op, and I somehow never had time to work the necessary hours to qualify me for membership. *Hmm*... Then, one day, Wife was done going to the co-op. Fairway and all its high-end, debt-stoking offerings had arrived in Brooklyn. I was cooked. So began the excruciating weekly trip to yuppie grocery Valhalla, Fairway.

The closest location to us abuts New York Harbor, which means it sees all the wind, snow, rain, pus (?), or whatever stressful conditions Mama Nature can cook up today. Between the lists, the texts, the calls, the forgotten items, or forgetting to bring the NPR totes, the whole process was often an emotional drag over concrete. Then COVID-19 happened, and suddenly, grabbing the eggs became a more dramatic proposition. Look, no matter where you stand on COVID-19, we can all agree that risking it all to get Mommy's Greek yogurt ain't it. And just as I was getting used to suiting up in my spiffiest hazmat onesie, Instacart went and entered the chat. For those of you who have successfully dodged targeted ads, Instacart is one of several popular apps allowing you to grocery shop from the comfort of your home (without the risk of life or lymph nodes). Of course, like most free-market solutions to big problems, like keeping the populace healthy and fed during a time of crisis, Instacart and other apps come with their fair share of issues, namely, that those fetching the food for you aren't making anywhere close to what Instacart management likely pulls down, so I am always sure to tip big (because I am a good person, which is literally the entire reason I wrote this book).

A few years after the pandemic's darkest days, I kept ordering via Instacart. This is not a plug for the app or the service. It's a plug for getting your time back. Now, if you want to take your choreplay to the next level (you do), here's the off-menu setting I made:

I joined Costco.

Note. I didn't say *go* to Costco. I said I *joined* Costco. Feel free to follow suit or join Sam's Club or Big Lots or Jimmy Joe's Food Emporium Wholesalers, Feed Lot, Wedding Chapel, Grain Depot, and Goat Disco. Whatever! Look, again, I don't know what's near where you live and I don't know your life, but I can speak to Costco.

Costco offers free delivery on orders over $75 (which is literally the cost of a Spanish onion these days). And to be clear, I am not a paid sponsor of Costco. I'm just using Costco as a shining example of how buying in bulk can save your life and shamelessly gunning for a brand partnership with a wholesaler that definitely does not have to be Costco, OK?!

But seriously, here's why you should do the big-buy thang, especially if you have the storage space. Not only will you save a bundle buying bulk on the price per unit, but (thank me later) you won't be running to the store all the goddamn time to pick up this, that, and the always-forgotten third. It will already be in the house. For instance, I haven't bought toilet paper in about a year. That's right. Jen and Ben were still married the last time I bought TP, and Diddy had yet to be MeToo'd. Yup, it was a different world, friends. All that to say, it's been a minute since I've bought the staples that had previously caused so much agita and so many curt text exchanges with Wife. I haven't bought paper towels since I don't know when, and there's never not milk or coffee, especially when I buy brew in three-pound drums like I'm running an area deli.

Look, maybe you're the kind of person who enjoys their weekly trips to the market, so ignore this if you want. But for me, it's just one more task in a schedule that's already frightfully overstuffed. Who wouldn't want to save time, money, *and* enjoy more goods? It's a deep-fried burrito of a win-win for a slothful cheapo like myself. To say nothing of the savings!

According to a study by LendingTree, the number stands at 5 to 10 percent saved annually on your grocery bills, which translates to $300 to $600 per year for the average shopper (which I am).[1] Additional research by consumer expert Clark Howard, published on his popular personal finance website Clark.com, tops out potential savings at $1,000 per year.[2]

I don't know about you, but that's a whole-ass weekend getaway with Boo right there.

THE CORTISOL OF IT ALL

The best part of buying in bulk is how much it dispels the tension brought on by scarcity. In the past, when we were running low on TP, things could get... messy (in so many ways). Now that's just not a thing (at least compared to the degree it once was).

It's wild to think how simply creating longer gaps between the conversations of "We're out of [enter staple here]" have led to more domestic tranquility. The cortisol levels decrease, shoulders lower, and jaws tend to unclench when there is enough of what you need on hand. Shouts, of course, to my guy Abraham Maslow and his banger of a theory, the hierarchy of needs, which argues that we as *hu-mons* have five levels of needs:

Level 1—Basic Needs: Food, water, shelter, your buddy's Hulu password

Level 2—Safety: Stability, money, working locks

Level 3—Community and Belonging: Relationships, friendships, Kiwanis Club memberships, cuddle clubs (or whatever curls your toes back)

Level 4—Self-Esteem: Self-respect, self-worth, aka that thing Gen-Xers weren't really born with

Level 5—Self-Actualization: Self-fulfillment, meeting your fullest potential, being one of those people who returns their library books on time like a champ[3]

According to Maslow, you're going to have a pretty tricky time living your most realized life if you are a bleached pile-o-bones 'cause you've died of starvation. Big facts. It's also worth noting that each ascending level of Maslow's hierarchy of needs depends on achieving the one just below it. So, it's little wonder your relationship harbors residual animosity if you're always outta eggs. Food is the whole game. To paraphrase Maslow, "no unsalted organic butter in the butter tray, no peace." Seems silly, doesn't it?

I tried sidestepping Mr. Maslow and his theory for years. I wondered why my relationship was always so buggy without ever considering the OJ levels—*know your levels!* When the milk levels are right, and there is enough Bonne Maman strawberry jam or *sel-za* (the price of marrying a New Yorker), Maslow says fulfilled relationships aren't too far behind.

This is so blood simple, and many of you may be shaking your head at what I'm offering up here, but we also tend to forget that humans are all at once complex and basic at our core. We have a myriad of emotional needs, and at the same time, if our brains don't get oxygen for three minutes, it's a fuckin' wrap! So take it from me. Get over yourself. Be like me and buy a ton of flour in the name of home-front harmony.

Quick story: My beloved tween daughter loves to bake whenever (and use up all the damn flour). This scarcity sends Wife over the edge. There's never flour when she needs it. As a result, Wife would get into it with tween daughter, and sometimes your man would catch strays, too.

Rather than suss out the nebulous issues involved, I just dropped two big bags of all-purpose flour on the matter. Yep, when the bag says "all-purpose," one of those purposes is settling family disputes. Since I brought a small silo of flour into the house, I haven't heard another thing about daughter's baking (except that she leaves a hot mess—but those raspberry scones, though!).

Scarcity is a trigger. It ticks us off. It means we have to spend money, which there never is enough of, and spend time, which is always in short supply, to correct matters. Allow me to get all sciency and say that scarcity also triggers our amygdala, which is the part of the brain that processes fear and stress. Think of it as that friend who's always catastrophizing. The last person you want in a lifeboat. The amygdala is out there doing too much. Yes, its job is to alert you to threats to your well-being so that you act and do something to neutralize said threats, but unlike your phone, the operating system never came up with an update. So, basically, we live in a very modern, high-tech world but respond to all its stimuli with a system that was likely last updated sometime well before the Ice Age. Yeah...

You don't have to worry about being crushed by a giant sloth anymore, and yes, these megafauna were once a thing and actually as tall as trees. But our old, dusty-ass amygdalas pretty much explain why my family goes into petit mal seizures whenever we run out of microwave popcorn. Now, I might lose a lot of you when I say I am six of one / half a dozy the other about popcorn. I could take it or leave it. But for the rest of my family, it's an essential part of their diet. Weary of the moaning, groaning, and *toldya so*'s whenever we were fresh out of kernels, I choreplayed it and went bulk on this, too. I bought a box containing forty-four bags of microwave popcorn (literally, ALL the popcorn) and haven't heard a peep since. Lord, they never tell you how sweet the silence of domestic tranquility can be.

KEEPING TRACK

As I have said many-a-page in this book, technology has caught up with the slob. There is no better time than now to give the bare minimum of effort around the house because the internet has *got you*!

When I do my weekly online grocery shopping, the moment I open the app or website, it already knows what I bought last week—because, yes, you're totally being watched, obveez! Then there are other sites that rhyme with *Spamazon* that offer subscriptions for household sundries at discounted rates. I only maintain one subscription, for my loving dog's food, which works like a charm. I can't remember the last time we ran out, except when my mother-in-law's dog found the dog food bag and ate more than fifteen pounds of kibble in one sitting. She's fun.... *We love her*...

But between the subscriptions and the tracking of it all, staying on top of the household is no longer the fate worse than death I once made it out to be. I say this as a man often winded after crafting a single email. So find your app, find your opposable thumbs, and pick a day to "go shopping." You'll find that you'll slip into a groove pretty quickly. Plus, as humans, we tend to eat the same things over and over again. Lean into that. Let big tech and its worrisome tracking software actually work for you for a change. Thanks, Big Brother! See you in the canned food aisle!

QUICK CAVEAT

Now that I've extolled the virtues of buying bulk online for home delivery, I can also say that I buy groceries this way only when I am buying dry goods, not produce. Turns out my family and I were never gonna knock out nine pounds of seedless grapes before they rotted. Lesson learned. Note: Buying bulk can be like taking a meat ax to your problems. There are times when you need a meat ax, but there are times when you don't, and understanding the difference is key. For instance, I buy dish soap, shower gel, TP, PT, spices, aspirin, bandages, maple syrup, honey, sugar, flour, and root vegetables in bulk because those things are either dry goods or they don't spoil quickly. Conversely, I avoid buying produce like strawberries in bulk because they go bad quicker than an idealistic politician.

I wish that this had been more obvious to my dumbass, but allow me to share it in the off chance no one ever told you: Don't buy a lot of what spoils in a week just because the price per unit is relatively low. Also, sometimes, you just need to run to the store and grab a couple of avocados. In that case, I don't order them for delivery. I go myself. Maybe it's flawed logic, but I can reasonably handle a quick ten-minute dash to the store for a few items. Reserve the online grocery shopping for weekly refills, not random top-offs. I can cover the rest myself, thank you very much.

YES, YES, GOOD, GOOD... BUT WILL THIS GET ME LAID?

A: Maslow left out a level in his hierarchy, so please allow me to add it. Based on personal experience and a study sample of precisely one person (Wife), I can tell you that anticipating and securing what food items your household needs won't discourage your person from bumping junk. I'd wager the opposite will happen. In fact, I would like to wedge this level into the amended hierarchy of needs right between "Safety" and

"Community and Belonging." Why? Well, yes, if you keep the fridge stocked, you can likely expect a fun romp in the spring linens, but not if there isn't a working lock on your bedroom door! That part...

JUST THE TIPS, PLEASE

- **Be prepared:** We're not talking doomsday-level, World War Z prepping here, but if you can swing it, having stores of home goods and staples will make for less stress.
- **Join the most exclusive clubs:** Costco and Sam's might not be the sexiest clubs going, but joining will save you time, money, and stress. And with online shopping, you can do it from anywhere... like your toilet.
- **Give your amygdala a break:** Our amygdalas love bulk and abundance. So to keep this part of your brain happy, make your next jar of mayo industrial sized.

FINAL BOSS LEVEL

YO! THIS IS THE LAST LEVEL OF THIS RPG WE CALL *CHOREPLAY*. Oh my. I barely have focus enough to read a cocktail menu, so color me impressed, friends. We've tackled quite a bit, but there's still more row to hoe (easy . . .). Here on the Final Boss Level, choreplay becomes a bit more metaphysical and complex. I didn't dub this section Final Boss Level for funzies! Now we get into the dark heart of the matter at hand.

We're saving the most intense parts for last (fun!), but you've got this. On Final Boss Level, I will guide you along my road to actively valuing my wife's concerns. You can only do better than I did! Trust. Also, this final section covers how to protect the choreplay gains you've made and how to deal with friends' and relations' responses to your glow-up. Finally, we will speak on the beast that is people pleasing and what it takes to committing fully to a life of choreplay. Gird your loins!

Chapter 11

BE CONSIDERATE, YOU INCONSIDERATE F**K!

AKA How I Am Learning to Drop the Nasty Little Habit of Downplaying My Wife's Concerns

WHAT IS IT ABOUT THE OLYMPICS? EVERY LEAP YEAR, THEY'VE got me in a headlock.

I go four years without thinking about the pole vault, the triple jump, the Fosbury flop, or who is the fastest person on Earth that is not Usain Bolt. And yet, every leap year, I watch this global showdown like I have money running on the outcome, which I certainly don't because life is already gamble enough! Sidenote: I am actually in a FanDuel TV ad, so I do think I'm one of the few people on Earth who has made money off of FanDuel without actually placing a bet—all this to say that I love the 4 × 100 meters relay.

More than the blistering speed of the sprinters, I marvel at the handoff. The handoff is the most pivotal part of the race. A good handoff can mean the difference between the ecstasy of Olympic immortality and the agony of also-ran obscurity. That handoff is everything.

THE RELAY

Shortly after Wife and I moved our growing family from a single-level apartment to a multilevel house, she started to do something curious. She would leave items at either the top of the stairwell or at the bottom. It struck me as rather odd. It reminded me of what guests do in a hotel when they leave the remains of their long-since-eaten continental breakfast, complete with spent mini Heinz ketchup bottles, outside their door for retrieval. What in the White Lotus was going on?! Why was she leaving clothes, toys, books, and soaps at the bottom or top of the stairs? Then I thought maybe Wife wasn't the culprit. At that point, we had a toddler and a rambunctious newborn, so there were a few possible suspects, and I didn't want to rush to judgment on this particular case. One day, though, I caught Wife red-handed leaving my son's toys at the bottom of the stairs.

I took her in for questioning like a scene from *The First 48*. And, yes, I interrogated her without her lawyer present, but I wanted to know why she kept leaving random stuff at the bottom and top of the steps. Turns out, she did that in the hopes that after straightening the house, *someone* (me) would take these items either up- or downstairs for her, as though she were handing off the baton in a relay. That was an eye-opener. I had no idea she left these items out, trusting that I would kick in and do my bit. At that moment, I felt so oblivious and out of touch. But did I change my ways henceforth until the end of my days?

Fuckouttahere!

Wife and I had this discussion about five years before the pandemic. (As I said previously, all it took for me to begin to change my ways was a global health crisis that killed untold millions.) When it comes to habit changing, I'm the little pinecone in Yellowstone National Park. All I need to grow into a giant conifer is time and the deadly heat of a horrific wildfire. That's all!

For a time, I wondered if my wife was the only person who did this relay thing.

Nerp.

At least according to my TikTok research and the gajillions of comments these relationship humor vids generate, it's pretty safe to say that what Wife does is not an isolated case. So, dear reader, as always, I will pay you the compliment of being blunt when I say that if you see any of the following items lying about—a full trash bag by the back door clearly bound for the garbage, clean sheets that belong in the linen closet, dirty sheets waiting for transport to the washer—do your relationship a favor and do not ignore. Grab and go!

Let me repeat that.
Grab. And. Go!
And whatever you do, do not drop the baton!

ALL IT TOOK WAS A GLOBAL SICK DAY

Wife is Marie Kondo's sister from another mister. If you don't know who Marie Kondo is, do not stress. In brief, Kondo is a professional organizer from Japan who blew into the zeitgeist in the 2010s and seized on America's popular imagination, to say nothing of our sock drawers. In her internationally best-selling book, *The Life-Changing Magic of Tidying Up*—whose title I so cleverly pinched for my subtitle—Kondo argues that happiness and life balance are but an organized broom closet or a spiffy junk drawer away.

Wife was already a paragon of tidiness when she read Kondo, but after she devoured her book, it's safe to say Wife became a full-on freak of neat. Forever after, she would arrange a random storage space and invite me to marvel at her handiwork. Minimalism, clean lines, *and* Lil' Kim tunes—these are the things that send Wife into shallow orbit. The mathematical harmony coded in symmetry and patterns sends her into a buzzy rapture that I struggle to comprehend. Obviously, Wife is functioning at a higher frequency than your man.

In open rebellion against Wife's hermetic sense of order, I defiantly maintained small and not-so-small groupings of loose clothes scattered about our room, which were a source of frequent domestic tension. Some mornings, dawn would break over the ridgeline of the clothes pile(s), and it looked something akin to a miniature version of the Grand Tetons at first light...but smellier. Hoodies long since forgotten were somehow entwined with funky, twinless socks and boxer briefs, creating a sartorial driftwood essence. There was often such a veritable array of textures and fabrics and funks that it nearly looked like a Bushwick installation piece titled *Derelicte*.

Sometimes a pile's sheer size would give me pause. If I were to clean my pile(s), where would I even begin? What did the floor even look like under there? I might as well have been dismantling a C-130 Hercules because I didn't know where to start.

I was not inclined to find out, either. And I always had the handy excuse that I was too busy to do anything about it. Plus, we had a cleaning lady who came every other Tuesday, I would tell Wife. Let her take care of it.

Let me just pause briefly here to say that, if you agree with this sentiment, please do your utmost to shoehorn your head out of your butt.

On a long enough timeline, this kind of stinking thinking just doesn't pay. Slobs cannot keep slobbing, looking for someone, anyone to keep house for us—be it our long-suffering partners or cleaning people. Sure, you can hire a cleaning person to tidy up after you. I did. But then, for whatever reason (the pandemic), our cleaning lady wasn't coming every other week. Yeah, checkmate.

I admit. I have a hard time letting go of old behaviors that no longer serve me (like they ever did in the first damn place!). Personally, I wish I embraced healthy choices sooner, but I don't. I always seem to hang on too long until the center cannot hold, and you have to leap. Anyone else? But that's me. I'm a recovering dilettante. I hate change. Recently, I came across an African proverb that sums up my MO to a tee:

When you burn a bridge, you'd better be ready to swim.[1]

Bars. I make mistakes. I wreck things. I shatter what I have built. And, yes, I can be too dramatic about it all, too (obviously). But...also, I can swim. That's not a metaphor. I actually can hold my breath for a really long time (#flex). But I can also change. I can adapt. I can overcome. That's in my LinkedIn bio. Every once in a while, I actually listen to my better angels—and so can you.

UNHAND THE CAN

OK, now that we've firmly established no one could be as emotionally immature / avoidant / passive aggressive as I was and still *somehow* remain in a functioning marriage, the time has come to broach the Final Boss Level of choreplay. And to do that, we of course need to talk about *The Simpsons*. What? I'm a latchkey kid raised on television; of course my opinions were forged by a bunch of former *Harvard Lampoon* TV writers.

In *The Simpsons* episode "Homer's Phobia" (season 8, episode 15), Homer gets his hand stuck in a vending machine. The emergency crew is called, and after a lot of commotion, one of the rescue workers asks:

"Homer, are you just holding on to the can?"

To which Homer sheepishly replies, "Your point being?"[2]

And that's me. I'm always holding on to that damn can. Anyone else? Whenever Wife and I would tangle about my mess (which wasn't infrequent), I'd find myself defending the indefensible. I found myself holding on to the can. Mama always said I was hard-headed. #Believethewomen.

In my running, years-long rhetorical war of attrition with my spouse, I'd argue at turns that "disorder is its own order!" (Preach!) Or "No one can be as Type A as you" (can I get a what what?!) or "All things eventually fall apart, right? That's the second law of thermodynamics" (which is super helpful!).

Kudos to Wife for not fully busting me upside my head in those moments. My parries were threadbare copouts, and after years of this mind-fuck malarkey, I'd ground my person down to such an extent that, at some point, she all but stopped asking me to clean up after myself. But why was I even resisting so much? No doubt scholars will debate this for generations, but the real answer for my insipid recalcitrance may well be because, at times, I can be what the French call "a giant knob." In my continued unwillingness to put away my clothes or clean up after myself, I was still at this late date acting out like a surly teen under my parents' roof. I would be damned if I was gonna clean my room, Mom! No one's the boss of me!

When I was growing up, an untidy room was grounds for punishment—a spanking from Mom or, worse, *another* spanking from Dad when he got home as if it were the most protracted version of *WWE SmackDown* ever. So, when I moved out of my parents' house, my disorder represented my rebellion. It was my tramp stamp, my tongue piercing, my stick-and-poke face tat of the cast of *The Golden Girls* because I just didn't give a flip (sad, I know). It was also a sign that this part of me, at least, was still mired in adolescence. But with each passing year, my mess became more untenable.

I mean, at this point, I had kids of my own. They have rooms, too! How can I tell them to clean their rooms if I'm not cleaning mine?!

My very precocious kids picked up on the dissonance and hypocrisy of it all way too quickly. In mixed company, the kids would throw their slovenly, rumpled father under the bus to anyone who would listen. They would say, "Daddy is messy.... Daddy's clothes are always everywhere.... Daddy doesn't pick up his things, so why should I?" And then I'd be like, "Kids should be seen and not heard! Ain't nobody asked you anything!" *Exhale.* Bottom line: It's not a good look to parent from a place of "Do as I say and not as I do." If kids see that being untidy is an option, they will take it.

I did. I spent far more time around my mother than my father. My mother is one of the most brilliant people I know, but her office was always a goddamn glorious mess. There were loose papers, old photos, books, tchotchkes, and Afrocentric ephemera everywhere. It was as cramped as the trash compactor on the Death Star but with fewer flesh-eating Dianogas or pesky hydraulic walls caving in on each other and way more warmth and heart. I spent a lot of time in that office. I saw that a person could function surprisingly well amid all the clutter and organized chaos. It's not surprising, then, I am as disorganized as I am. And if that's the price of spending that much time with someone as wonderful as Mom, that's OK. I've overcome it. I'm a grown-ass man well into his forties with a mortgage and am Level Two certified in choreplay. Even if my mom did model disorganization for me, it's time to let that go. At this point, I'm focused on running a tight ship so that my kids can see that it's possible. As Mom has always said, "Jordan, if you were organized, you'd be dangerous." It's time to live up to that. Love you, Mom.

KNOW WHAT YOU'RE FIGHTING

I'm gonna come up for air and momentarily cease with the self-deprecation to say that what I love about my relationship is that my partner and I fill different roles. Although Wife can teach my kids all about the benefits of a lifetime of organization, education, and civic engagement, there are other areas where she would tell you that she wouldn't make the best of role models. Unlike her square-ass Urkel of a husband (there

I go with the self-deprecation again!), my dear wife won't be able to school our kids on the perils of teens having fun with controlled substances. Ain't no way! We are different people like that. And really that's OK. She is a product of Brooklyn in the 1990s. I am a product of SimCity suburbia.

For a long time it baffled me that Wife, who hails from one of the grimiest places on the planet, could be so supremely tidy. Had she ever gone outside?! There are whole-ass trash tornadoes in the middle of the street. For too long I laughed off her need for order in a place as chaotic as New York. Finally, committed to taking Wife's concerns more seriously, I stopped dismissing or diminishing Wife's neat-freak tendencies long enough to realize how our different upbringings factored into our respective values.

For kids back then growing up in 1990s NYC, drugs were basically ranked among the four food groups. As she and I have discussed, I will be taking point on the DARE portion of the parenting program, and she will be covering... pretty much everything else. That is, until our kids become adults and want to know how best to twist a nice fatty with a filter to boot. She can do that with one hand. It's kind of a turn-on.

That Wife survived growing up in this very intense era in NYC's history is something of a miracle. At that time, teens frequented notorious late-night warrens like Limelight and the Tunnel (on school nights, no less!), and tweens traipsed into R-rated movies like they were Pixar films. By contrast, my upbringing was a tad more staid. I grew up in the tony suburbs of Dallas. Everyone's lawns and hedgerows were trimmed and green. It was quiet and boring AF, and though folks are moving there now because the city recently decided to cultivate an actual vibe, I wanted out! But back to my wife and her vibrant childhood! My much better half was birthed at home on the kitchen table and grew up in a rickety Brooklyn brownstone. Her hippie parents took on tenants to pay for the place, so there were a lot of random people in and out of the house. There was music, noise, clutter, and Wife was just a little kid trying to make sense of all this.

To negotiate this sensory overload, Wife—who happened to share one room for years with her sister and two brothers—always kept her cramped little space (whatever there was of it) immaculate and spot inspection–ready. In ways, she's still that little kid. Any mess in our house is triggering. Don't miss a trash night unless you want your ass served back to you in assorted pieces. I've known my wife's backstory for a long time, and until recently, my response to the anxieties she has surrounding cleanliness and order was to joke about it and to tell her to "lighten up."

I see now that my tack wasn't helpful. Maybe I was right that she should chill out sometimes about tidying up (I am), but being right isn't everything. Here's what experience in the game has taught me: For any relationship to truly hum, it's imperative to stop putting your head around your person's baggage and instead just put your arms around it... in a very loving, judgment-light embrace.

That took me too long to figure out.

Easier said than done, of course, but I invite you to start looking into your partner's relationship to tidiness *pronto*. What does it mean to them? What's their tidiness (or other obsession) origin story? For Wife, tidiness was a bulwark against a crowded/noisy house, chaos, uncertainty, and fear. Neatness is such a trauma response that Wife's college best friend would prank her by laying orphaned socks across her bed and then delight in Wife's subsequent meltdown. Wife is that Type A. She's that person who checks in to a hotel and can't do anything else—not even grab a complimentary beverage on the goddamn sunset mezzanine—*until* she unpacks her things and puts them in their respective spaces. But that's how Boo unwinds, and (deep, healing breath) that's OK. I'm done trying to roast her about it. It doesn't pay.

In the same way messiness had been my rebellion against a life of strictly enforced tidiness, tidiness remains Wife's middle finger to her forced bohemian past. With the exception of a very few pieces around our house, you can miss her with the rummage sale finds or the antique shop acquisitions. Perhaps it's an overcorrection, but for the most part, CB2 and Restoration Hardware are her jam. Clean. Simple. Spotless. As far away from hippies and djembe circles as possible. As I figured out, this is precisely why mess is so stressful for her. It brings her right back to those crowded conditions—family on all sides, walls—no joke—collapsing.

Our pin-neat little home is Wife's dream realized. It's order, on her terms. At some point during the pandemic, with so much time on my hands, I finally understood her and thereby understood *it*, and in so doing, I reframed why I clean up. Whereas, before, I was cleaning because if I didn't, Wife would be cross with me, now I was cleaning because I finally understood how triggering and anxiety-inducing this could be for her. And I love her.

Growing up, Wife shared one room with her three siblings. Any order in that environment had to be intentionally carved out. With that many little kids in so little square footage, I now see that she wasn't only vying for her own little patch. She was vying for a sense of self, too. I think that's a pretty powerful motivation.

Who knew Wife's motivations behind hitting the corners with the Swiffer went that deep?! Look, no one could be slower than me when it comes to seeing all of their person, but I'm just happy I was able to do it in time. The sooner you *embrace* what makes your person tick, rather than rationalize, judge, diminish, or upend, the better. And I doubt the reason why your person keeps her space organized (radicals for parents who were a bit more concerned with saving the planet than home decor) is likely the same as mine. If I had a dollar...

But I can tell you it's worth finding out.

CLAWING BACK FROM THE BRINK OF RELATIONSHIP OBLIVION: A HOW-TO

If you've been paying attention, you know that I've had a tortured relationship with tidiness. I've been loath to change my ways. However, I'm ultimately down for a reframe, especially for the sake of my mate. And as I've found, playing chicken may have its place in geopolitics, Mexican standoffs, or Texas Hold 'em, but bluster won't get you far in a relationship.

Don't put your person in the awkward position of "My way or the highway," unless you really want to hazard coming home one day to find your precious air fryer and the rest of your stuff strewn across the lawn or even torched Angie Bassett–style in the driveway with a menthol seesawing conspicuously from the corner of her mouth.

Also, making a relationship work in the long term doesn't take going belly-up like you are a floppy-ass Goldendoodle at the first sign of conflict, but it does take groping around in the dark for a different path that can still deliver a happy-to-happyish compromise. Hopefully, it can be done without going overboard. Former Secretary of State Henry Kissinger once said, "A good compromise is one where both parties are equally unhappy." Yikes! For a lot of reasons I won't go into (Vietnam, Laos, Watergate, getting rolled by one Silicon Valley con artist, Elizabeth Holmes, etc.), please don't take any advice from the late Henry Kissinger.

I'm here to tell you that the key to a more harmonious home isn't just doing the dishes on your assigned night. If only it were that simple. I mean, look, you could strike a nice little groove with the chores schedule and all, but that's not going to motivate a slob like myself long term. We're all the way at Final Boss Level choreplay, though, so I'm going to tell you what actually worked for us: I stopped seeing tidiness as a chore chart and started seeing it as a love language. Not mine, but *hers*.

I'd always noticed that based on optics alone, you'd never think Wife is from Brooklyn. She looks like a total Cape Cod WASP (but approachable, LOL), and it's only when she lays on her brassy, get-back New Yock accent that you think, *Uh, who are you? Who are your people?* I remember when she brought me to the house she grew up in. I was shocked, *shocked*! I was like, "You grew up here?!" I was confused. Her aesthetic was J.Crew, but her childhood home was *Sanford and Son*. By that time, we were already spending the night at each other's respective places, and she was already commenting on how my apartment looked like it had been raided by a government agency hell-bent on uncovering mislaid state secrets.

Yet, after all these years, here we are. She's as tidy as I am sloppy. But despite our Felix and Oscar *Odd Couple* pairing, we have made it work. That is to say, we haven't found a way to merely coexist. We found a way to thrive. And I'm happy to report we didn't have to do it by divvying up responsibilities and chores, either. Of course, if that's what it takes, more power to you, but I feel like embracing my person's origin story has created a more grounded way to relate to her need for order. Once I understood where Wife was coming from, the fight over dishes wasn't about dishes anymore. When I straighten up now, I'm not just cleaning—I'm showing up for my person. I'm saying, *I see you, and I respect what makes you feel safe.* We didn't need a spreadsheet of chores to make it work. We needed curiosity. And empathy. And maybe a Costco-size tub of Windex.

So, if you're stuck in your own domestic standoff, here's the solution: Stop keeping score. Start getting curious. Figure out what order means to the person you love, and see if you can love them *through* it—not in spite of it.

And, y'all, if I can reframe, *anyone* can. Take it from a guy who used to think "compromise" meant Wife finally seeing things my way.

JUST THE TIPS, PLEASE

- **Look for batons:** Does your partner leave "batons" around the house and are you picking them up? These are subtle and not-so-subtle signals for your help. They could also be batons! Again, I don't know you.
- **Make it personal:** It never hurts to understand the why behind your partner's tidiness MO. Find out and let it motivate you more than any chore schedule ever could.
- **Stop diminishing:** If your partner comes to you with an inconvenient want, fight the urge to downplay its importance. That is the work of an asshole.
- **Let go of that can:** Remember, sometimes our seemingly worst issues can be resolved by letting go of that metaphorical canned bev.

Chapter 12

PROTECT YOUR GAINS

SO YOU'VE MADE IT THIS FAR. IMPRESSIVE...MOST IMPRESSIVE! You've changed some habits and stuck to them, but how do you know if you're making any progress? Patience, my sweet summer child.

Luckily, other people will let you know—especially your dumbass, trifling-ass friends.

I recently caught up with an old buddy of mine from comedy. While we were trying to find a time to meet up, I told him I could be free around 8:45 p.m. that evening, since I was planning to cook and wanted to help put the kids to bed too ('cause that's who the eff I am now!). This did not go over well with my friend. He said, "Can't you just tell your wife to cook and meet me at seven?" Sure, I could, but did you hear what I just said?! My friend, whose wife and kids were out of town that week, complained that he had to drive an hour or more from Jersey to Brooklyn to see me and that he would have to eat dinner alone before we met up. I know, right? The horror. Why didn't I just drop everything, then? Not dinner alone!

In years past, that's exactly what I would have done. I would have wrapped my need to please in the guise of "bros before hoes" and peaced-out on cooking. But it was a new day; I'm Final Boss Level. This is my final form! And I had to protect my gains.

Though it killed me a little, I told my friend I couldn't meet him earlier. He was not pleased. My heart started palpitating, but then . . . the moment passed. I had created what some cultures refer to as a "boundary." And against all odds, I kept the boundary! I didn't cave. It only took forty-something years to get there! What a rush!

Yes, part of the reason I didn't want to drop my plans to cook was that it would undoubtedly upset my wife, but that wasn't the sole reason. Ostensibly, that seems enough, but again, I'm trying to convey that at some point, I had to draw a line. I couldn't be out here trying to please both my friend and my wife. If I cook only to please or to avoid conflict, it will only lead to resentment. As dumb and inconsequential as it might sound, I wanted to change my relationship to my responsibilities. I wanted to stop seeing them as drags on my psyche. Yes, chores can be a lot, but aside from the rare man-eating dishwasher, they likely won't kill me. And by finally leaning into them, they became much less daunting and odious.

Chores are never light work for me, but they lose their teeth when I do them enough. They've become part of my routine—not an encumbrance or a heavy load. Yes, sometimes I need reminding to do them, but we all need reminders. Chores haven't changed. What's changed is my attitude toward the mountain. I know I am now equal to the daily challenges that a marriage with children presents. Planning isn't as exhausting as it once was. I'm in better physical and emotional shape now. I'm up early these days. I have a jump on the day. I see more moves ahead than I used to. For once, I am the hammer. For once, I have time. I feel more in control than I ever have. It's a very new sensation for me. This is my first foray into self-possession, and it does not suck.

I am a fantastic sidekick, and much to my surprise, I've become something of a sidekick to myself! That supportive energy I so freely crop-dusted on anyone with a heartbeat I've begun to turn inward, and holy hell! I love how game I am about myself. These days, it's all "What are we doing today, Jordan? What do *you* want to do, Jordan? How are you feeling, Jordan?" I'm not saying that I don't need friends—I do. But, damn, I never knew how much of a friend I could be to myself, too.

As for my dad friend, we met up at 8:45 p.m., whereupon he complained till last call about his wife and how he never wanted to move to Jersey. My very unprofessional opinion is that my friend could use some of my hacks. Because all during our "conversation," he complained about his wife's need for order as overblown and dumb. I couldn't help but cringe. He sounded just like me. I don't remember every drunken catch-up session with my friends, but this one will stay with me for a while. Until very recently, I was *that guy*, grousing and griping about my wife, never considering what role I play in the marriage, and getting that much closer to the end.

In the past, I would join in on these bitching (can we say that word anymore?) sessions, but this time I found that I no longer had the appetite. Why? Because something had shifted. I found myself just wanting to be home with my wife, not having beers with my cranky dad friend moaning about how annoying his spouse was and inviting me to throw my wife under the bus too. I couldn't fake that I was as miserable as he was, because I wasn't... so I didn't. I listened politely, drank my beer, and kept it moving. Just remember, you don't have to brag about how good you and your person have it, but you also don't have to pretend that things are worse than they are just to fit in. As a pleaser, I've done that too!

If you're happy and you know it, be that.

Here's a pro tip to protect your gains: Do not post or otherwise share all of them. Try having a secret for a change. By posting or running your mouth, you might then feel the need to live up to a certain image, which is a trap in and of itself. Do not fall for it. It's your journey, and no one else's. Just remember: Zero people (who ultimately matter, anyway) are keeping score. This is your story; frankly, it will be over all too quickly, so consider not spending it worried about whatever notes your friends have for you.

Now, your friends support you in many ways, but there are limits to everything. This is when you must listen to your intuition (and *me*! Just kidding.). Sometimes, it's better to keep your own counsel on something like switching to healthier life habits. Besides, if you get your life together and glow all the way up, even if you don't tell a soul, *there will be signs*, and people can/sometimes do feel threatened by them.

I remember when my daughter was born. At the time, I had a very close friend in comedy. We were basically bros from other Joes. When my daughter Izzy arrived, my wife and I went MIA. We had a baby now, whereas we didn't have one before. Things had changed! You'd think my buddy would be reasonable about this life change, right? Not the case. Zero chill detected.

Instead of hitting us up on the baby registry, my friend fired off an angry email straight to my forehead. I'm paraphrasing here because getting through the entire message without punching drywall was hard, but my friend was opining that I had abandoned him for my dumb baby. Yeah, he really sat down at a computer, well into his thirties, and wrote this. And though this happened in 2013, this was my first inkling that our closest friends—ones you depend on to be unflappable, if not reasonable—can sometimes be jealous little brats. I mean, this friend of mine was actually jealous of a *baby*. He wasn't checking on the baby or asking how the delivery went, which had its share of difficulties.

During the delivery, the doctor who administered my wife's epidural botched the shot. When my wife returned home after the delivery, she began experiencing headaches so severe that we had to take her back to the hospital. We soon discovered she was leaking spinal fluid—yikes! What followed was a hasty-ass apology from some bigwig doctors at the hospital and a none-too-comfortable spinal tap and patch for my wife to stem the leaking spinal fluid, aka that stuff your brain floats in!

So imagine getting my friend's dumbass, self-serving, self-absorbed message at that moment. I still think about this messy blip on my timeline every now and again. I am a huge proponent of chosen family, but be advised: Sometimes our chosen siblings can act like jealous twins. Be forewarned: When we start to change, our friends' and loved ones' insecurities can come into plain view.

For instance, though I am getting in shape, what I certainly don't do is post a daily stream of content about my fitness. I post at most one or two vids per month about my workouts (thirst trap!). Yes, I am human, so vanity plays at least a small part in why I post—aka the only reason to do anything!—but I was knocked sideways when a friend went out of their way to knock me and my dumb little workout reel. They said I creepily looked into the camera at one point, and that is true, LOL. I did look like a bit of a creep when I made the fateful error of looking at the camera for a nanosecond during the video. But this friend then went on to say that *everyone* these days was starving themselves (in order to get in shape), the implication being that I was an irredeemable basic for even exercising. They waxed on and on about it, like they were a junior senator filibustering against a massive spending bill. They popped all the way off!

I respect and love this person a lot. I considered taking down the video. Was I being too insensitive to them? Then I thought about it for a moment. I hadn't committed a crime (beyond looking like a goddamn snack!). While I was focusing on my friend's feelings, I hadn't thought about mine at all (because fuck me, right?!). Don't get me wrong—again, I love my friend. But this experience taught me that people can be selectively supportive. Whenever we experienced commercial success, they're right there for us. We toast with countless drinks. But when it came to another type of success, which they found "narcissistic," they weren't as happy. These are the moments when we must protect our gains and let our less evolved friends (sorry) wallow in their misery.

BUILDING COMMUNITY

I loathe when people put the two words *building* and *community* together, but here we are. It feels forced AF and usually comes after you sign up for a gym membership or some wellness service with a hefty price tag. Why are we always encouraged to create community but only *after* you cross a paywall? If I miss a payment or my debit card gets declined, will I be unceremoniously exiled from the "Jam of the Month Club" community? I fear my poor heart couldn't bear it.

Let me go out on a limb and say that community that doesn't have a paywall is likely going to be stronger than those contrived as a feature of late-stage capitalism. I know I'm blowing minds here, but one of the most effective ways to find your people is to scroll through your contacts and reach out to your friends. Reach out to people for whom it's been a minute. Suggest a hangout, but leave sports and/or business out of it. Remember when we were kids and we would just hang out with our friends? Why do we stop doing that? Kids don't need a reason to see their friends other than just missing the other one's face. Novel, I know.

Somewhere in the fog of adulthood I certainly was disabused of that. Suddenly, status became the key determinant of who I chose to spend my time with. I socialized chiefly to network, hoping to leverage myself into ever more exclusive circles. In brief, it wasn't worth it. I should have been hanging out with my actual, longtime friends—not glamorous strangers I hoped to win over. What a waste of time.

Lucky for me, I still have a few teeth in my head and a few grounded people in my life I can call friends. So, if you're going to build community, work with the paints on the palette. That's what your contacts are for. Get over yourself and reach out to that pal you admire, not the one you endure. Let them be a good influence on you. You've come too far to ruin what you've built by spending time with somebody toxic.

Next, if you want to build community, literally do that. Volunteer when and where you can. With all of this newfound energy, I was struggling with where best to direct it. Turns out, I thrive in steamy church soup kitchens. I guess it reminds me of my choirboy days. But maybe soup kitchens aren't your bag. If you're a parent with school-age children, volunteer at their school or join the PTA, bake some goodies for a bake sale, be that poor schmuck at the dunking booth who likely contracts listeria for giving up his Saturday. It's a small price to pay for codifying your gains.

In my experience, the best way to avoid relapse is branching out. No, I didn't start a dad crusade or a Facebook group of like-minded slobs, and I'll tell you why: First, that sounds like a lot of work; second, I'm not a crusader. I'm just a guy who happened to find a seat when the music stopped.

INTEGRITY: AKA HOW TO CHECK YOURSELF

But how do you *maintain* healthy habits? Great question. I'm glad I continue to ask banger after banger after certified banger.

The best way to keep up with choreplay is by maintaining your integrity. And the best way to keep your integrity is to do what you're supposed to be doing when no one is watching. In effect, you're watching the watchman. By definition, that's what integrity is: doing what you ought to without being asked, urged, or prodded.

Integrity is a muscle, and a practice. Doing the right things can be difficult when there's no immediate feedback loop. If there's no cheering section to applaud every time I empty the bathroom trash receptacle, why even bother? If no one witnesses every time I empty the dishwasher, do I feel a bit sad inside? Obviously. But that's beside the point. The point is that your home is as much your home as it is your partner's. The more I clean my home, the more I invest in creating my own standards of cleanliness and organization. Yes, I can have them, too! So, do the dishes, give *yourself* an attaboy, and keep it moving!

If you have trouble congratulating yourself for your efforts, allow me to share a recent eureka moment that helped me start looking inward for validation for maybe the first time in my entire adult life. As I said, I go to predawn workout classes. It's a breezy mixture of weightlifting, Vinyasa yoga, cardio, and some Pilates thrown in, too, that leaves me with a feeling like I've been trucked by a charging water buffalo and then blown from a cannon (that's not what you think it means). Sometimes the ~~grand inquisitor~~ instructor will parse out compliments to students in this class about their form. Admittedly, I live for these compliments. They can make my day. To me, they are evidence that I am getting stronger and improving. Sadly, I think it only fair to tell you sometimes I will add a bit of flair or theatrics to try to get their attention and get those coveted kudos. And now you know. Anyway, I'm sharing all this because one day as I was balancing on one foot while executing narrow rows or some such nonsense, I didn't get a compliment. Thirsty me did not get the encouragement I thought I was owed.... I remember nearly asking aloud, "Can she see me? Can she see me?" Also, just to paint the picture, this is a heated class. At a minimum, the room is heated to at least ninety-five degrees. So at this point sweat is coursing down my back and arms. It dripped into my eyes and my ears. Amid this strain and elevated degrees of difficulty—hell yeah!—I wanted my teacher to see me. I wanted their recognition. And then suddenly another voice from somewhere down deep bellowed, "Do *you* see *you*?" And a shiver ricocheted down my vertebrae. My nostrils flared and I immediately felt a tide of emotion wash over me.

It felt like, through all my efforts, all my choreplay routines encompassing my spirit and body, something broke through, permeated the mantle of my consciousness, and snaked its way to the surface. For the first time in my life, I wanted to know if I could see my own efforts. All it took was over two hundred 6:00 a.m. classes, but it happened. That's all. Internal validation didn't come quickly for me, so please don't become discouraged if yours is as slow coming as mine. Hopefully, your breakthrough isn't as dramatic and doesn't cost as much in gym fees as mine did. But now whenever I'm feeling thirsty, I ask myself that question: "Do you see you?"

YOU NEED CLAY TO MAKE BRICKS

There is one mantra I will offer you for swimming this far out from shore. "Brick by brick." I say that to myself every day, especially in those tough times when I want to throw in the towel. And when I want to quit and blow up my life, I acknowledge that and also listen to that other voice in me that says to keep pushing, to keep building—brick and mortar, brick and mortar. I will allow that there are points when I think that I won't make it through the day. At times, I'm living minute to minute, moment to moment and the siren call of self-destruction and self-pity seems all too irresistible. Maybe I'm in an intense morning workout and I want to cut and run. Maybe I'm in a squabble with Wife or with my offspring. Maybe I'm reading headlines (don't do that!). Whenever that dark pall descends, I fall back on my mantra like a king to his keep and repeat "Brick by brick. Brick by brick." So far. So good.

JUST THE TIPS, PLEASE

- **Set boundaries like a boss:** Saying no may feel akin to hari-kari, but saying yes to everything just might make you an undercover misanthrope. As trite as it sounds, you're really pissed at yourself. Your friends and family are just catching strays 'cause you never learned to say no.
- **Chores aren't a prison sentence:** Turns out, doing the dishes won't drain your soul—just your sink. Whenever I get down about washing my dishes, I just thank my maker for the food that he's provided me—especially eggs! Those bad boys are so pricey they should be kept under glass.
- **Not everyone loves a glow-up:** Some friends cheer for your wins…until your win makes them feel insecure. Protect your peace. Your growth may create displacement, but it's up to your friends to find their place in it, not yours.
- **Keep your joy on the DL:** Though haters are telltale signs you're doing something enviable, consider not broadcasting your happiness like it was press day. Pick a win today—big or small—and celebrate that solo. See what that feels like.
- **Integrity is cleaning like no one's watching:** If I take out the garbage and no one is around to see it, did it happen? Turns out, yes! Be your own audience.

Chapter 13

F**KIN' DO WHAT YOU PLEASE, PLEASE

IF WE WERE IN A VIDEO GAME RIGHT NOW ('CAUSE THE SIMULATION is so real, bro!), we would be entering the penultimate board. Wow. We've come a long way in this book. We were kids when we started. So, I get it: You're drained. Your thumbs and trigger finger are zapped. But don't hit the pause button now. Time to storm Final Boss Level of choreplay's sanctum sanctorum. Finish strong. Be proud. You're reading a whole-ass book in 2026. That said, let's get into it.

My descent into shameless pleasing began at a random KinderCare in Texas in the early eighties. I mean, who can't relate to that? I must have been about four or five at the time. Part of my school had burned in a fire (we don't talk about that!), and as a result, my parents had to put me in KinderCare temporarily.

So there I was in KinderCare—essentially the Dunkin' Donuts of childcare chains, which caters to the trend of dual-income households brought on by the women's liberation movement. With Dad and Mom out of the house making paper, someone needed to watch the crumb-snatchers. Enter: KinderCare.

Anyway, a mountain of rightly burned bras later, there I sat in a red-roofed, franchised pre-K, just trying to make the best of it. I don't remember much from my time there except that I hated it. My school friends weren't there, and I was too old, really, to be in day care. These were little kids, and at all of four years old, I was a grown-ass man by comparison.

Then, to make matters worse, there was this one kid at KinderCare who was going all the way through it! Every day this kid cried ceaselessly—hot tears, bawling, moaning, lips aquiver. It was brutal. The worst part was that none of the workers at this KinderCare would comfort this obviously troubled child. No one would soothe him. They just let him sob until he coughed and choked on his own tears. After days of this, I couldn't take it anymore.

I walked over to the little boy and started making silly faces. He smiled! He laughed! The tears stopped. Suddenly, he was OK...*or so I thought*. Thinking the little boy was finally content, I walked away to amuse myself with some Duplos that needed my attention.

Wrong move.

The moment I did that, the boy started crying all over again. Unable to bear his tears, I entertained him again. And so it went...for weeks. I entertained the little boy all day. I did the work of the KinderCare staffers for them. I put my toys to the side and kept that little boy happy, tap-dancing for his amusement. That was the moment I became an unrelenting entertainer and a wanton pleaser. It was also the moment I became a sidekick and a second banana—someone driven in large part by the desire to keep the peace and manage other people's emotions, since I only felt safe depending on other people's emotions. Yeah, not an ideal way to live!

I would take this toxic trait into every one of my relationships that followed. Friends and lovers would gun it down the highway of life astride their metaphorical Harley, and I would ride in the sidecar...*if it so pleased them.* It was exhausting. Never did I ever stop to figure out what I needed or vocalize my needs. I stayed in friendships, relationships, gigs, and situations that no longer served me for way too long for fear of upsetting others. When I broke up with someone or quit jobs or even moved apartments for something better, I was wracked with paralyzing guilt.

Being such a bootlicker kept me from taking risks and big swings. It hobbled my ability to assert myself or challenge others for jobs and gigs. Sometimes, I'd run into fellow entertainers who'd say, "You took the part I wanted." After I heard this enough times, I let it eat away at my self-confidence. Did I take what was plainly not mine to have? I guess so…

Of course, someone with a healthy sense of self (not me) would clock that for the malignantly narcissistic nonsense it is. *I* took the part from *you*? Seriously, fuck off. If you've ever said something like this to someone—even as a joke—don't. You sound like an entitled brat. In the private sector, we ain't owed shit. In an industry where—forgive the graphic language here—you eat what you kill, all bets are off… except if you're me. Then everyone's happiness is your job.

Of course, my dumbass knew better and I *still* wanted to appease people who would say it to my whole face. I hated being the author of anyone's pain, so eventually, I started prepping less for auditions, shrinking in interviews, finding the middle. Dimming my light so I wouldn't draw fire. I didn't want to "take" anyone's job. They seemed to want it more. Maybe they deserved it more. Who was I to stand between them and what was "theirs by right"?

At that time, a big part of me believed that what was most important was to be liked, maybe even more than booked. I never wanted to be envied, resented, or disliked and would do practically anything *not* to be, even if that risked taking myself out of the competition. After a while, I made peace with a pretty constant diet of rejection. Sure, I missed out on money and opportunities, but at the very least, it made someone else happy. If I wasn't working, that meant someone else was, right? Win-win (????).

But when I did experience success, when I got jobs or gigs, I hated the flak that came with it. I didn't want trouble. I just wanted to soothe that metaphorical toddler while the KinderCare staff took an extended smoke break and sucked down Virginia Slims in the adjoining blacktop parking lot. I couldn't stand the least bit of conflict. I wanted friends, relationships, and career success, but not if it came with a downside.

Pretty counterintuitive, right?

Some would call it fucking dumb. And they would be right.

I DON'T EVEN LIKE EVERYONE

I've done therapy and I meditate, but sometimes, it's a random bit of conversation that you catch between two people on a subway platform that truly transforms you.

One snowy winter's day in Manhattan, when the trains were running especially slow (when are they not?), I overheard two ladies working out all the problems of the world. They were older—seasoned and hardened by the realities of life in New York City. Still and all, these two had each other. I can't recall the exact content of their conversation, which is just as well since I should have been minding my own damn beeswax, but sometimes eavesdropping like my name is Amazon Alexa has its benefits. Here's what I recall (to be read with thick Brooklyn accents):

Friend 1: I don't know why she hates on me so much. What did I ever do to her?

Friend 2: I don't know why you waste your time worrying about that.

Friend 1: I know...

Friend 2: No, you don't know. Listen, I know you damn well don't like everybody. *Why in the hell does everybody have to like you?*

Damn. Lady, whoever you are, thank you for saying that. If you're reading this (why would you?), your words hit me like a full deployment of bunker-buster truth bombs. Target destroyed... and built back up again.

Now whenever I feel myself slipping into my filthy habit of putting others at ease at my own expense, I think of her words. I certainly do not like everyone. In fact, I don't like a majority of people and some animals—mostly man-eating sharks because they are godless killing machines. Sorry not sorry, PETA. So, why *does* everyone *have* to like me? Such a good question, and a very self-evident one at that.

Not feeling the pressure to be universally beloved is likely among the more freeing things I've ever felt before. The charms of others don't always work on me, so why should my charms be any different? Aren't we all acquired tastes (unless your name is Dolly Parton or Zendaya, and you have literally zero haters)? It was only when I decreased the amount of tap-dancing I did for others and increased the amount of tap-dancing I did for myself that things started to change.

Trust me.

BOTTOM LINE

Pleasing yourself risks displeasing other people. A book with a subtitle like mine is probably not the place to do this, but fuck it. I'm going to go ahead and quote abolitionist Frederick Douglass here. He said, "Without struggle, there can be no progress." And much like a savory condiment, that quote goes so hard it can be applied to so much, including the pursuit of happiness. Yes, your happiness could cause friction, but deferring your shot at happiness for peace will only lead to resentment.

And just remember, in life there is no good time for anything. My friend and hilarious comedian Dan Ahdoot has this very funny joke that no one in real life has ever said: "This is actually a great time to break up! Now I can finally learn to play the flute." It doesn't work like that.

If you set yourself up to be "Mr. A Hundo-and-Ten Percent," expect people to think of you that way. Don't be surprised if going rogue and putting yourself first ruffles some feathers, especially yours. It happened to me. My taking up space didn't go over well with my friends and loved ones. It was an adjustment.

But, overall, the results have been better than expected. It turns out that when you seek to please yourself and, in so doing, happen to displease others, you don't die unless—as I've feared—you're somehow an undead subfunctioning zombie and don't know it (it's possible). You'll likely find, though, just as I did, that the world continues to turn and that eventually your loved ones and friends adjust right back. Of course, while I'm doing it, while I'm actively pleasing myself (get your mind out of the gutter) and doing whatever I feel, my emotions are mixed all the way up. So learning to listen to your intuition, to trust yourself, believe in yourself, and—most importantly—deliver for yourself is no Swiss picnic.

(Let's break it down / make it easier / you're not alone etc.)

Anyway, if you're now thinking, "Cool rant, but how the hell do I actually start putting myself first without becoming a full-blown monster?"—buckle up. The next part breaks it all down: how to be a little bit selfish, please yourself on purpose (again, not like that), and maybe piss off a few people along the way. Don't worry. You're not the only one out here fumbling through this. I got you. Let's get into it.

MICRODOSING SELFISHNESS

Momentarily inconvenienced people are my drug of choice. I get a dopamine rush anytime I bring anyone Prometheus fire of information or aid and comfort they in no way asked for. Anytime I can reveal to the temporarily benighted how the

New York City subway system works, which way is east, or the difference in hours between Eastern and Mountain time zones kinda steams my jeans a little bit—not gonna lie. Up until recently, I have swooped in to fix whatever was momentarily bothering literally anyone. But recently I've made something of a compact with myself to redirect this energy inward. I'm not going to stop being that guy. I'm just going to start being Mr. Helpful for me first before others. Easy, right?

Recently, while out running errands I spotted a tourist couple exploring my neighborhood with a paper map (!!). First, I didn't know they made those anymore, so I definitely wanted to randomly insert myself into this scenario. Second, in the past, I would have likely become these people's personal tour guide, smoke-jumping into their cute mini-crisis, then triaging and pointing out my area's myriad hidden gems, including my neighborhood's Michelin-rated restaurant, Tanoreen! Look, the restaurant is great and more than lives up to its rating, but I'm just too goddamn much! All that to say, it took every fiber of my being not to show these people around, even though I had a to-do list and zero time to do so. But I just love being a search engine in a meat suit.

Clearly, this young, nubile couple would have eventually cleared whatever speed bump stood in their way without my help. Why did I have to be so outwardly solicitous all the time? Why couldn't I be as solicitous and pleasing to myself as I was to capable strangers?

THE HARD PART

I wish someone had told me how lonely being even a little self-focused can be. For me, it has been a whole second puberty of sorts, but without the "backne." In the past, I would fill my cup with other people's issues so that there would be precious little time left for mine. It was a very effective albeit self-destructive way of avoiding what was on my plate. Now there is more time to focus on me, and whether you're an extroverted introvert like me who is so good at small talk because I actively avoid conflict like a New York native avoids Times Square or you're an irredeemable extrovert who can't stand the thought of perhaps being disliked pretty much *ever*, one thing remains a constant: You get your time back, *yikes!* All of this endless time can be a lot. And whereas before, when I could blame other people with their high-maintenance lives for soaking up so much of my time and energy, I can no longer use that excuse that *they* are the reason I couldn't get my shit together. *Gulp!*

And let me just say, sitting with myself and my gonzo thoughts, getting a lot of my time back made me feel stir-crazy. Without the distractions from my friends' concerns and myriad dramas, I was able to observe how long it took me to do… pretty much anything. In the before days, nothing was too important for me not to respond to my friends' texts or calls. I was kind of like an emotional chain-smoker except the smoke was all secondhand. Deep, I know…

The biggest surprise that came with focusing a spotlight on myself was how much less time it took to do my work when I wasn't dedicated to figuring out my friends' issues. Turns out, it doesn't take you days to churn out a pitch deck when you're not deliberating how to respond to the newest half threat / half love-letter DM from one of your famous friend's followers or when you're not bringing your buddy's girlfriend Persian food on a random street corner because he did her dirty but he's out of town and you don't know how to say no! When you're not doing things like that, work becomes that much more of a breeze.

BUT HOW DOES BEING MORE OF A SELFISH PRICK SERVE MY RELATIONSHIP?

Learning what you like and what you're into and what your specific preferences are can only work to burnish your relationship. Because if you know what you like, then you know what you dislike, and my great hope for you is that you will not suffer in silence about this but rather voice it.

Learning what blows out our metaphorical Afro puffs and what turns us on creates a sense of self separate from our person. For instance, have you ever hung out with someone, and all they talked about is their wife and/or partner? Don't get me wrong. I adore Wife, but I don't want to talk about her all the damn time! When your partner or spouse or kids become your identity, it's not a good look. It betrays how truly enmeshed you are with your person, so much so that you can't think of another topic to discuss besides them. Being that selfish prick has helped me foster a sense of self, something I had all but abandoned since that fateful month at KinderCare.

That said, here's a small caveat. If you change enough, expect your person to notice, and expect questions, too. My shift toward positive self-interest has been as much an adjustment for my partner as it has been for me. It's only fair for your person to even wonder aloud the timing and motivations behind your journey. Why in the free world are you switching lanes now?! Why aren't you bending over backward for everyone like you usually do? Isn't that your brand? Answer: Because choreplay wasn't a thing until now, mmk?! Also if you're anything like me, you chronically procrastinate about literally all of it. For instance, I used to go a remarkably long time between shaves and haircuts, so much so that once when I came home with a much-needed shearing a few years back, I scared the bejesus out of my toddler son, who ran to his mother because he thought I was a stranger pretending to be his hitherto scruffy-ass dad. Bottom line: There will be ripples on the water, but the trick is to weather them. They will subside eventually.

Doing the work of intentionally making more space for myself and not being a walking help desk comes with a load of positives and its fair share of issues, too. I really did not know how much of a mantle I was shouldering in my role as "Mr. 110

Percent, aka Mr. Doing the Most." I'd been expending so much emotional labor and energy on total strangers that should have been reserved for me (or at least people I actually knew). When I was out here trying to save the world instead of confronting my own issues, it felt like the emotional equivalent of sweeping all my baggage under *your* bed. Eventually, whatever we put under there is gonna start to stink/attract ants (metaphorically speaking, of course).

There may well be momentary pain or discomfort as a result of me unapologetically pursuing what makes me happy, but long story short, nobody died. I'm not hurting anyone or doing anything criminal. Life is too short to be an emotional hibachi chef, putting on a nonstop show for others' amusement, catering to their needs only. To me, I'm better off upsetting Wife from time to time rather than pleasing her all the time. These days, I don't let my wife's hypothetical displeasure dissuade from what I want to do. I do it, come what may. Is it perfect? No. Sometimes it's downright onerous. But it's also past time for this to happen. It's also wonderfully honest, which is something my relationship has been missing.

And that's the source code of choreplay. It's the courage to have an honest, imperfect relationship with your person because you're having a more honest and genuine relationship with yourself. You're doing the most for you. You're doing more for you, and if you're like me, you're learning that deep down your person actually likes this for you. Turns out, a little swagger looks good on you.

So now, when I catch myself slipping into old habits, bending over backward to keep everyone happy, I think back to that subway conversation. I don't like everybody—why should everybody have to like me? That simple truth has saved me more times than I can count. It's kept me from dimming my light, from riding in the metaphorical sidecar, from tap-dancing myself into exhaustion. I'm still unlearning, though. I'm still figuring out how to put myself first without feeling like I'm breaking the law. This journey started with me desperately trying to be a better partner (or else). I didn't know it would end up making me feel like a better version of myself—a better friend to myself, a more engaged parent, aka pretty much all the things—and did I mention the sex!? And, yes, I'm so old I use the definite article *the* to describe the sex like it's in limited supply. In any event, I am happy to report that lately this boring dad is crushing (my wife, but still!).

And if the world can survive my mild selfishness, maybe I can, too.

Chapter 14

PUT YOUR WHOLE ASS IN OR GET YOUR WHOLE ASS OUT

OK, THIS IS WHERE I LEAVE YOU. THOUGH I AM A BIT TORN, SINCE it likely should have been where I started this whole book. Why? Any change, large or small, commences with commitment. That's pretty self-evident in the abstract, but not always as clear when it comes time to stand and deliver IRL.

For instance, whenever I tell a new joke, my demeanor changes, my voice pitches up and warbles like I'm a zit-spattered pubescent teen. The senses, once loose and flowy, sharpen to a steely point, and I suddenly become aware of every movement as my butt cheeks clench all the way up! *Too much? Well, at least you know that about me now.*

In these moments, I always tell myself that I can resume my regularly scheduled program of self-contempt and latent anxiety after the show. But come what may, I commit to the joke. I lock in. I lean into the premise and sell the punchline with everything I've got. Sometimes the audience's reaction is an explosion of laughter. Other times, a polite chortle. Sometimes moans. Sometimes nothing. I will take nothing over moans, of course. No matter what, I always lean in like my name is Sheryl fucking Sandberg. And even when a new joke beefs it like a certain unlucky bear cub RFK Jr. admittedly stashed in the trunk of his car and then dumped in Central Park 'cause he was late for a flight (as normal people do), I don't immediately throw that joke on the great ash heap of unwanted material.

Before I give up on a new bit, I'll usually try it on an unsuspecting audience about eight or nine times (OK, fine—closer to twenty; I have a complicated relationship with letting go). Turns out, abandonment *and* approval are two of my longest-running costars—I introduced you to my need to please in the previous chapter. Update: I'm actively working on this dynamic duo, both in and out of Zoom therapy, where my therapist just nods like, "Yes, and?"

Oftentimes, I hold on to jokes out of fear that I'll never come up with anything as funny again, so I better find a way to make it work! Not the healthiest way to operate, I admit, but here we are. Maybe I'll try the bit with a different tone or a different setup or perhaps a new punchline. This trial-and-error phase is level: critical to my creative process. Even if the audience is all but breaking out in hives from discomfort, I will still try to expand on any viable part of the joke till it grows like a sourdough starter. I will experiment and test the material again and again and again until I stumble on a way to break through and connect with the audience. And when I do connect, I use that tenuous toehold to go about coming up with another joke building off this newest bit. That's the discipline.

And that's what a fifteen-, thirty-, or sixty-minute stand-up performance is, really—an assembly of once new and unproven ideas that have been nurtured into something deserving of laughter. Good jokes are rarely born fully formed like bumblebees. Good jokes wobble on spindly legs and need to learn to stand on their own with no small amount of devotion, humiliation, and care. *Can this guy serve up an animal metaphor or what?!*

For me at least, I do my best work in comedy when I fully drop into the moment. When I don't worry about the comedian that's gone on before me or the person who is going on after me or if the crowd is restless or tight or crammed with drunken brides-to-be (yuck!) or campers or Mormon missionaries or even folks in town for a furry convention (that's happened), I thrive. When I stop judging myself and start embracing myself, I shine.

I have always understood that commitment is critical to success in comedy, but when it comes to relationships, I never fully grasped its necessity. There was something of a blind spot there. In fact, I remember joking to whoever would listen that there were whole months or fiscal quarters when I felt as if I were on relationship autopilot (yikes!). For a long time, I thought that was some pretty cool shit to say. Now, I wish you all the breeziest of relationships, but if you find yourself out here flexing about the fact that you and your person are on autopilot, please know at that juncture you're likely headed for Trouble Mountain. Never get *too* comfortable. Stay engaged. That's Final Boss Level choreplay. Believe it or not, I was sort of proud of how inert my marriage had become. I somehow thought detente was proof of a healthy bond. After all, we weren't fighting, right?

Instead of pouring myself into my marriage, I was going through the motions of holy matrimony, but for a good thing to last, it takes being wholly matrimonial. PS, I don't know if I used *matrimonial* correctly there, but we've come too far to change it now and, given the context, it kinda fucks.

In my marriage, I was like a hack comedian who does the same stock jokes over and over again with no feeling or passion, no commitment. I don't allow myself this kind of emotional detachment in my professional life, so why was I OK with it in my marriage? Because deep down, every hack comedian knows that they are afraid to truly put themselves out there—because in doing so, they risk the humiliation / searing pain of rejection. Pre-choreplay, I was a hack of a husband, and I knew it.

GET OUT NOW

Wife never had trouble committing. She's just like that. It's rare for her to quit (for better or worse) once she engages. She doesn't do anything halfway. She doesn't sample. She doesn't browse (unfortunately). She pours herself into everything she does. It's her superpower. In part, it's how she graduated with honors from Smith College. It's also how she helped found a competitive high school in Brooklyn, how she attained her PhD while successfully taking on the city hall to win our kids' school unique dispensation when the school board tried to mandate a new reading curriculum that she knew to be trash on arrival. Not just *any* city hall, either. Again, we are talking about the New York version, which we all know is level: bananas! When she locks in, it's a fresh pita *wrap*.

I wish I could say the same about me, but for much of my adult life, I've been a fence-sitter. There have been moments when I actually have locked in and those moments have made my bones rattle like castanets. Moments like my wedding, moments like the birth of my two beautiful children. At these times, I wasn't one foot out. I was both feet in. I wasn't worried that eventually Wife would wise up and figure out that she'd married a well-meaning ass (but an ass nonetheless). All this to say (and stay with me here), if you don't feel like you can fully commit to your person, get out.

Now, before you finger-roll this cute little book into the *basura* (trash), let me say this:

Sometimes a relationship cannot be salvaged, especially if *both* parties cannot fully buy in.

I hesitate to call any romantic relationship a waste of time, especially if that relationship results in kids or life lessons of one stripe or another. But if you aren't sure you can fully vest in your bond, especially if you exhibit a fateful pattern of bootlicking and people pleasing, look around for the exits. Take it from me, you're imploding and self-immolating, only in slow-mo. Apologies for being so dramatic about it, but the fact is that, unless you really feel like you can rebuild the car as you drive it on a rickety-ass bridge, maybe consider other options. There will be pain, to be sure. Between friends' and family members' breakups, I've had floor seats to the trauma. Is it a fate worse than death? No. Is it raw-dogging a cross-country red-eye on Spirit Air levels of bad? Getting warmer.

There is no shame in winding down a relationship after many years of trying to make it work. On a long enough timeline, the inefficiencies inherent in a dysfunctional Rube Goldberg machine–type relationship may prove untenable. In this case, listen to your intuition. It's gotten you this far, right? And here's the most important part. Even if you implement all the tips and hacks I've offered up in this book (I gave you some gems!), and you end up splitting with your partner, guess what: Choreplay will help you in your next relationship. Choreplay will make you a solid catch, in this relationship or the next.

HALL & OATES

Wife and I were out the other night. The kids were having a slumber party with their cuzzos, and we had a whole night to ourselves. After a morning of omega Boss Level choreplay, including but not limited to a predawn workout, coffee and pastries for Wife, kids fed breakfast, all before putting in a full day of keyboard pounding on my MacBook Air, I was twenty-five minutes late to our exciting dinner date.

Wife was hot. She tore my *tokus*. She hates a wait. I was hurt, though. I didn't feel like my tardiness was my fault at all. I'd left with what Beyoncé's internet told me was more than enough time to arrive to the sceney downtown eatery. But Google can't account for what a beat-down public transit worker is gonna do. In the end, I was at the mercy of the public transit, and the public transit was falling down on the job (no surprises there!). Now, everyone knows that the New York City subway system is a disaster, but I wasn't taking the subway. Nope. My dumbass was trying be cute. I was taking a ferry. Yep, I was on a damn waterway, where the boats have literal *miles* of free space ahead of them, and New York still found a way to make me nearly a half hour late. Thanks, New York!

No one wanted to hear all this less than Wife. She just gave it to me—both barrels / full clip. Did I fire back a battery of invective? Not *this* time. Why? Because, as I said, being right is a lot, but it's not the whole game.

After a tense beat or two (and a stiff drink), relative bonheur was restored when I told her the following: "Alina"—OK, Wife's name is Alina, it's time you know—"Alina, you and me, we're like Hall and Oates. We may not always like each other, but we're definitely better together than we are apart." She just laughed. I was back in, baby! But I wasn't back because I said something clever. I was back because she wanted me to be back.

All the tasks I'd done for our family (and for myself, for that matter) were the cake. The joke was the icing. Lately, Wife can't stay mad at me as much as she did before. And it's not because I somehow got more adorable.... How could I get more adorable, y'all?! Nope, it's choreplay. I pray that I will get to spend the rest of my days in my marriage. Whatever happens, I am confident I have made the most of this undeserved last of the last, random, loose-change-between-the-seat-cushion of chances.

No one knows how long they will have with their person (unless they're to be burned at the stake for heresy at dawn), but whatever time I do have will have been worth it. Since I began my choreplay journey (apologies), I fell in love with myself. I learned that I love me some Jordan! I learned that the more I cleaned up *my* act and controlled what I could control, the better it got with wife. Knocking out chores has made me a better mate, a better friend, a better sibling, and a better dad, too. In fact, helping out with the chores has made my relationship anything but a... chore (couldn't help it). With love and hope I leave you with this:

> The last chapter, the final act in the gender gap saga cannot be written until couples share more. And until the world of work makes that a less costly thing to do. When different-sex couples give up couple equity they increase gender inequality. When couples increase couple equity, they advance gender equality.[1]

Bars... but as a comedian, I gotta leave you on a laugh, though. So here's one of the oldest relationship jokes in recorded history. It's a banger dating all the way back to 1900 BC Sumer:

> Something which has never occurred since time immemorial: a young woman did not fart in her husband's lap.[2]

Amiright, ladies?! Look, love with all your heart. Hold on to your person with both hands (around their hips), and tip your waitstaff. Good night!

JUST THE TIPS, PLEASE

Finale

- **Don't blow it!:** Kidding! Skip to the next one.
- **Commit to the bit:** When it comes to long-haul relationships, life imitates art.
- **Don't get too comfortable:** Relationships require our attention, so tweak, refine, and lock in.
- **Pick your battles (or at least bring a joke to them):** Being right feels good, but it ain't everything. If you can't win the argument, at least land a solid one-liner before surrendering.

Afterword

MORE PLAY

THERE REALLY IS NO GUIDEBOOK FOR BEING THE CIS, STRAIGHT male partner out here trying to reignite a relationship's pilot light with a dying cell phone and wet matches... so I wrote one! I know that the advice I proffer in this book is depressingly simple, but this is our world. I didn't make it. I'm not trying to run it. I'm just trying to stay married to my person. And in case I'm wrong, and there is another book out there aimed at redirecting dumb, well-meaning dudes from divorce, let a brother know! I'd love to read it. It would have spared me a ton of time, trouble, and co-pays!

To my great surprise, my foray into choreplay has been chock-a-block with discovery and revelation. Like, I didn't know I was allowed to be a morning person. I didn't think I could get in shape and stay in shape. I didn't know that I could make my clothes pile(s) recede at least somewhat. I certainly didn't know that in the process of rebuilding and rejiggering my operating system, I would not only rekindle my sex life with

Wife (yes, please!) but also, for the first time since I was a kid, like myself. How could I know that, ultimately, I would grow to enjoy my own company and take much more significant gaps between self-loathing? I haven't given up on self-loathing completely, of course! Never that. It's likely too ingrained at this point. Plus, if I *never* hated myself, I think I would risk becoming more unbearable than I already am. PS, I know I'm not intolerable, but I have to say that kind of thing so I don't come off as a whole and complete dong.

When you're as butt-deep into marriage as I am, folks typically look for relief and guidance in therapy and therapy alone—as well they should. For my marriage, at least, choreplay has worked as an effective pairing. Put another way, choreplay has become, as they used to say in breakfast cereal ads, "part of a well-balanced (therapeutic) diet." Do we still fight? Absolutely! Wife is a Brooklyn lady. For Brooklyn people, *everything* is grounds for argument. They are just hot-blooded that way. As a culture, they love to debate, and there is nothing I know of on which they have little to no opinion. They argue bagels, pizza, and which street has the most rats. If you're wondering, it's East Fifth Street in the Village. Sorry!...My New York in-laws say they don't like to argue, and *yet* that's all they seem to do. So, suffice it to say, Wife and I still argue, but we don't argue about chores to the extent that we once did. #Progress! These days, instead of fighting about the dishes, we commiserate and worry that our kids aren't washing their dishes enough (I wonder where they get that from). Bottom line: I am no longer as much of an obstacle to tidiness as I once was. These changes have made a difference.

Now, for the biggest surprise of all. Before choreplay, I couldn't pass a day without some message care of Wife asking me to grab one thing or another at some point during my wanderings. She'd ask me to grab more milk, eggs, paper (toilet or printer or both), or any other item that could possibly inconvenience me that day, or so I thought. That was the before times.

Recently, I found myself asking *Wife* to do the same. I'll never forget the first time I asked her to do it. Wife was out at some chic nightspot with friends, and I was at home packing the next day's lunches for our children ('cause I'm a goddamn hero, y'all!). In the process of preparing lunch, we ran out of Pepperidge Farm Goldfish crackers, the manna to children and scourge of rear car seats everywhere. Since I didn't want to leave my young ones alone to dash out to the store, and I didn't want to order something so small on my phone, I texted Wife to grab Goldfish on her way home. I found the text exchange. It went like this:

Me: Would you mind grabbing goldfish on the way home?
Wife: Who dis?

Suffice it to say she forgot to grab the Goldfish. *Ruh-roh* … Don't worry. We survived. Wife returned home from her sexy mom sesh, boozed up, and very much in the mood to smash. And that's really where I wanted to be in the first place, anyway.

Thanks, choreplay!

ACKNOWLEDGMENTS

There is no way I could have finished this without my brilliant editor, Niyati Patel, and everyone at Grand Central Publishing. Niyati, you are a juggernaut, and though we have never met IRL, I live in the hopes that we one day will. I'd also like to thank my agent, Robert Guinsler, for believing I had a book idea in me. Turns out, I did! Who knew?! I want to also acknowledge the unwavering support of my die-hard assistant, Olivia Levine. I cannot believe how very lucky I am to get to work with you every day. Also, special shout-out once more to my mother for pushing me to up my writing skills, and to one of my favorite economists, Nobel Prize winner Claudia Goldin. Her writing and work on the topic of gendered roles within the household were true inspiration. To my children, for being such miracles of personality, intelligence, and warmth, I thank you. I love you more than life. Finally, I am so happy to thank my wife, Butch aka Alina aka my best friend, the smartest, most beautiful woman I know.

NOTES

Epigraph: Long Friday

1. Eliza Reid, *Secrets of the Sprakkar: Iceland's Extraordinary Women and How They Are Changing the World* (Sourcebooks, 2022), 8–10.
2. Reid, *Secrets of the Sprakkar*, 8–10.
3. "The day the women went on strike," *The Guardian*, October 18, 2005, https://www.theguardian.com/world/2005/oct/18/gender.uk.
4. Thomas Nilsen, "'What Now Happens in the World Is Utterly Awful,' Vigdís Finnbogadóttir," *The Barents Observer*, October 29, 2016, https://www.thebarentsobserver.com/security/what-now-happens-in-the-world-is-utterly-awful-vigdis-finnbogadottir/123497.
5. Sif Sigmarsdóttir, "Once More, Iceland Has Shown It Is the Best Place in the World to Be Female," *The Guardian*, January 5, 2018, https://www.theguardian.com/commentisfree/2018/jan/05/iceland-female-women-equal-pay-gender-equality.

Introduction

1. Centers for Disease Control and Prevention, National Center for Health Statistics, "FastStats: Marriage and Divorce," last reviewed March 17, 2025, https://www.cdc.gov/nchs/fastats/marriage-divorce.htm.
2. Shelby B. Scott, Galena K. Rhoades, Scott M. Stanley, Elizabeth S. Allen, and Howard J. Markman, "Reasons for Divorce and Recollections of Premarital Intervention: Implications for Improving Relationship Education," *Couple and Family Psychology: Research and Practice* 2, no. 2 (2013): 131–145. https://doi.org/10.1037/a0032025.

Chapter 1: Invisible Work

1. Gus Wezerek and Kristen R. Ghodsee, "Women's Unpaid Work and the American Economy," *Economics Review*, September 1, 2022, https://theeconreview.com/2022/09/01/womens-unpaid-work-and-the-american-economy.

2. Nehal Aggarwal, "Women's Unpaid Labor Is Globally Worth $10.9 Trillion, Report Says," *The Bump*, March 6, 2020, https://www.thebump.com/news/unpaid-labor-women-global-national-value; and Clare Coffey, Patricia Espinoza Revollo, Rowan Harvey, Max Lawson, Anam Parvez Butt, Kim Piaget, et al., *Time to Care: Unpaid and Underpaid Care Work and the Global Inequality Crisis*, Oxfam Briefing Paper (Oxfam International, January 2020), 10, https://doi.org/10.21201/2020.5419.
3. "Claudia Goldin: Biographical. The Economist as Detective," Nobel Prize, https://www.nobelprize.org/prizes/economic-sciences/2023/goldin/biographical/.
4. The Notorious B.I.G., *Ready to Die*, track 10, "Juicy," produced by Sean "Puffy" Combs and Poke, recorded 1994, Bad Boy Records.

Chapter 2: Mask On

1. Bruce Springsteen, *Darkness on the Edge of Town*, track 5, "Racing in the Street," recorded March 1977–March 1978, Columbia Records.

Chapter 3: Assess Your Mess

1. Donald H. Rumsfeld, "DoD News Briefing—Secretary Rumsfeld and Gen. Myers," news briefing, US Department of Defense, February 12, 2002, https://web.archive.org/web/20160406235718/http://archive.defense.gov/Transcripts/Transcript.aspx?TranscriptID=2636.
2. 1 Corinthians 13:11 (King James Version).
3. Martin Scorsese, *Pretend It's a City*, episode 5, "Department of Sports and Health," featuring Fran Lebowitz and Spike Lee, Netflix, 2021.

Chapter 4: Executive Function

1. Marco Hirnstein, Frank Larøi, and Julien Laloyaux, "No Sex Difference in an Everyday Multitasking Paradigm," *Psychological Research* 83, no. 2 (2019): 286–296, https://doi.org/10.1007/s00426-018-1045-0; and Julien Laloyaux, Frank Laroi, and Marco Hirnstein, "Women and Men Are Equally Bad at Multitasking," *Harvard Business Review*, September 26, 2018, https://hbr.org/2018/09/research-women-and-men-are-equally-bad-at-multitasking.
2. André J. Szameitat, Yasmin Hamaida, Rebecca S. Tulley, Rahmi Saylik, and Pauldy C. J. Otermans, "'Women Are Better Than Men'—Public Beliefs on Gender Differences and Other Aspects in Multitasking," *PLOS ONE* 10, no. 10 (2015): e0140371, https://doi.org/10.1371/journal.pone.0140371.
3. Leah Ruppanner, "Women Aren't Better Multitaskers Than Men—They're Just Doing More Work," University of Melbourne, August 14, 2019, https:

//findanexpert.unimelb.edu.au/news/2988-women-aren%27t-better-multitaskers-than-men-%E2%80%93-they%27re-just-doing-more-work#; and Leah Ruppanner, Francisco Perales, and Janeen Baxter, "Having a Second Child Worsens Parents' Mental Health: New Research," The Conversation, December 16, 2018, https://theconversation.com/having-a-second-child-worsens-parents-mental-health-new-research-107806.

4. Jennifer Baxter, "Mothers' Employment Transitions Following Childbirth," *Family Matters*, no. 71 (Winter 2005): 11–17, https://aifs.gov.au/sites/default/files/jb(4).pdf.
5. Leah Ruppanner and David J. Maume, "Why Couples Sleep Better in More Gender-Equal Societies," The Conversation, July 8, 2018, https://theconversation.com/why-couples-sleep-better-in-more-gender-equal-societies-98547.
6. *Global Gender Gap Report 2020* (World Economic Forum, 2019), 11, https://www3.weforum.org/docs/WEF_GGGR_2020.pdf.

Chapter 5: Ask Mom

1. Eve Rodsky, *Fair Play: A Game-Changing Solution for When You Have Too Much to Do (and More Life to Live)* (Sarah Crichton Books, 2019).
2. F. Scott Fitzgerald, *The Great Gatsby* (Scribner, 2004), 40.
3. *White Men Can't Jump*, directed by Ron Shelton, Metro-Goldwyn-Mayer, 1992, DVD.

Chapter 6: The One Where You Face That You're Not a Kid Anymore

1. Dr. Seuss, *The Cat in the Hat* (Random House, 1957).

Chapter 7: F**k Self-Care

1. Mark 12:31, New Revised Standard Version (NRSV).
2. *The Lord of the Rings: The Fellowship of the Ring*, directed by Peter Jackson (New Line Cinema, 2001), 1:31:25, HBO Max: https://www.hbomax.com/movies/lord-of-the-rings-the-fellowship-of-the-ring/fb9f961f-6302-4776-91d7-f1b7a69fb61d.
3. His Holiness the Dalai Lama and Howard Cutler, *The Art of Happiness: A Handbook for Living* (Riverhead Books, 1998), 71.
4. Marcus Tullius Cicero, *On Duties* (*De Officiis*), trans. Walter Miller (Harvard University Press, 1913), book I, section 70.
5. *Predator*, directed by John McTiernan, 20th Century Fox, 1987, film.

Chapter 9: Go the F**k to Sleep, You Sleepless F**k

1. Christoph Randler, "Proactive People Are Morning People: Proactivity and Morningness," *Journal of Applied Social Psychology* 39, no. 12 (2009): 2787–2797, https://www.academia.edu/3603579/Proactive_People_Are_Morning_People1_PROACTIVITY_AND_MORNINGNESS.
2. Attributed to Mark Twain, origin unverified. Quotation widely cited, but not found in Twain's known works.

Chapter 10: The Incredible Bulk

1. Davis, Maggie, and Dan Shepard. 2025. "Buying in Bulk Could Save Shoppers 27% on Average." LendingTree, August 19, 2025. https://www.lendingtree.com/credit-cards/study/bulk-buying/#:~:text=Many%20bulk%20shoppers%20estimate%20they,upfront%20costs%20of%20bulk%20buying.
2. Clark.com Staff, "How To Save $1,000 in 15 Weeks," Clark.com, December 7, 2022, https://clark.com/save-money/save-1000-in-15-weeks/.
3. Abraham H. Maslow, "A Theory of Human Motivation," *Psychological Review* 50, no. 4 (1943): 370–396, https://doi.org/10.1037/h0054346.

Chapter 11: Be Considerate, You Inconsiderate F**k!

1. "When you burn a bridge, you'd better be ready to swim," common proverb of unknown origin, widely circulated in modern usage.
2. *The Simpsons*, season 8, episode 15, "Homer's Phobia," directed by Mike B. Anderson, written by Ron Hauge, aired February 16, 1997, on Fox. Rescue worker to Homer: "Homer, are you just holding on to the can?"

Chapter 14: Put Your Whole Ass In or Get Your Whole Ass Out

1. Claudia Goldin, quoted in Christy DeSmith, "Nobel Winner Sees an Unfinished Quiet Revolution," *Harvard Gazette*, December 12, 2023, https://news.harvard.edu/gazette/story/2023/12/goldin-accepts-nobel-during-ceremony-in-stockholm/.
2. John Joseph, "World's Oldest Joke Traced Back to 1900 BC," Reuters, July 31, 2008, https://www.reuters.com/article/lifestyle/worlds-oldest-joke-traced-back-to-1900-bc-idUSKUA147851/.